T0053354

To:

From:

Praise for *Pressing Pause*

"With so many devotionals on the market, how do you decide? If you're a mom, the decision is easy. This is the one for you. *Pressing Pause* overflows with fabulous, practical, equipping, and sometimes even challenging, devotions. Waking up with this treasury of devotions will be a great encouragement to any mom!"

—Wendy Blight, Proverbs 31 Ministries' First 5 Writing Team and author of *Living So That: Making Faith-Filled Choices in the Midst of a Messy Life*

"*Pressing Pause* is a balm to a mother's soul. Through Karen's and Ruth's transparency and real-life stories, they make the truths and principles of God's Word come alive. This is definitely a treasure that all moms should have."

—Courtney Joseph, author of the book *Women Living Well* and founder of GoodMorningGirls.org and WomenLivingWell.org

"Just one moment with Jesus is enough for our hearts to be transformed forever. *Pressing Pause* creates a space for this type of life-changing encounter to take place. In this collection of thought-provoking and heart-mending truth, Karen and Ruth have created an opportunity for women in any stage of life to meet with Jesus. Surely there is no sweeter thing."

—Becky Thompson, mom blogger at Scissortail Silk, author of *Hope Unfolding*

"*Pressing Pause* is perfectly portioned for busy moms. Ideal for a morning devotion or a quick perspective shift in the middle of a crazy day, Ruth and Karen understand the challenges of motherhood and speak right to the heart with truth, humor, and hope."

—Kat Lee, speaker, writer at InspiredToAction.com

"Too often moms get caught up in the daily chaos of managing home life, work, and children. Ruth and Karen meet their readers where they are in the hard reality of life—gently leading them to a God who waits to sit and give them rest."

—Sandra Maddox, founder and coordinator of Treasured Moms at Saddleback Church, author of *Tiffany and the Talking Frog*, and blogger at theartofdomesticity.com

"As a stay-at-home mom of two toddlers, I often feel overwhelmed by the expected and not-so-expected events of each day. Laundry, meals, diapers, naps, tantrums, and housework all team together to steal joy. And if I'm not careful, the wonderful blessing of shepherding hearts can begin to feel like a chore. *Pressing Pause* has been a refreshing resource for me. The devotions are short, yet powerful reminders of God's truth, no matter how I may feel in that moment."

—Jami Throne, wife and mother of two

100 Quiet Moments for Moms to Meet with Jesus

KAREN EHMAN
& RUTH SCHWENK

ZONDERVAN®

ZONDERVAN
Pressing Pause

Requests for information should be addressed to:
Zondervan, 3900 Sparks Dr., SE, Grand Rapids, MI 49546

ISBN 978-0-3103-5779-7

Authors are represented by the literary agency of The Fedd Agency, Inc., P. O. Box 34173, Austin, Texas 78734.

Cover design: Milkglass Creative
Interior design: Lori Lynch

Printed in China

23 24 25 26 27 /GRI/ 23 22 21 20 19 18 17

To Suzy, who showed me how to be a mom who loves, studies, and memorizes God's Word. —K. E.

To Sandra, my faithful friend and mentor who inspires me to be a woman after God's own heart. —R. S.

Contents

CONTENTS

Introduction

Hey mom. Yes, you! Put down the frying pan. Stop folding the laundry. Quit thinking about what you need to thaw for supper or that project you're behind on at work. It's time you pressed pause. In fact, it's crucial that you do.

The book you hold in your hands is a work of our hearts. As busy moms in the trenches just like you, we know how hard it can be to find time to be alone with God to refresh your soul and recharge your spiritual batteries. With all the responsibilities of running a home, raising children, working, volunteering, and also trying to find a little time for ourselves, often our personal spiritual growth gets placed on the back burner.

It is our prayer for you that the pages of this devotional will serve as brief daily retreats from the busyness of life. Soak in the Scriptures. Experience the stories. Apply the practical principles. Let the words be massaged into your heart, helping you to press the pause button on life. Find and replace—find your concerns and replace them with God's promises. Recalculate—navigating to a new and healthy perspective. And then go forward in confidence as you tackle the tasks of motherhood.

A frazzled mom makes for a frenzied family. In this crazy season of caring for your family, don't forget to care for yourself as well. Take a few moments to meet with Jesus and create some calm in the midst of the chaos. Put the coffee pot on. A break from the busy is headed your way.

In His incredible love,
Karen and Ruth

Turning Worry into Worship

Karen

She is clothed with strength and dignity; she can laugh at the days to come.

—Proverbs 31:25

I think I have the worry gene, and I'm sure I got it from my mother. She passed down to me her aqua-blue eyes, her slightly crooked smile, and her tendency to worry.

When I was a teenager, I thought it was strange that my mom couldn't go to sleep until I got home. Then I got married, became a mom, and then years later, my children became teenagers. And guess what? Now I do what my mom did: sit on the couch appearing to watch television while my mind rehearses the quickest route to the hospital.

We moms can find endless reasons to worry. Kids. Marriage. Finances. Health. Relationships. The future. If we let our thoughts run wild, we can concoct all sorts of terrible scenarios, all starting with "what if." *What if my husband gets laid off? What if my aging parent needs to live with us or move into a nursing home? What if my teen makes a bad choice? What if something is wrong with my baby's development?*

Over time I've noticed something about worry: 99 percent of my past fears never came to pass. However, I spent oodles of time fretting about them. How I wish I could redeem that time and do something productive instead! What if I had turned my worry into worship?

Contrast my attitude with the woman in Proverbs 31:25: "She is clothed with strength and dignity; she can laugh at the days to come."

There's no weariness in her thoughts and actions. She laughed at the days to come—not in a careless sort of way, but with a confidence that came from God.

Because she wore strength and dignity due to her faith in God, she had a smile on her face and laughter in her heart when she considered the future. She trusted in God, whose faithfulness in the past assured her He would work out circumstances in the future.

God can use our tendency to worry to grow our faith. As we learn to turn our panic into fervent prayer and praise, trusting God's plan and timing, our relationship with God will be strengthened. Each time we turn worry into worship, we will find it easier to laugh at the days to come, like our Proverbs 31 sister.

God knows our future as well as He knows us. Our act of trust is to seek to know Him more as we place our future in His hands.

Oh, and to laugh a little more often.

Dear Lord, help me turn my worry into worship, believing that You are in control of the future. May I rest in Your loving arms, knowing You have my best interests at heart. In Jesus' name, Amen.

- What are your three greatest worries as a mom? List them.
- Take each of those three worries and pen a prayer to God instead.

Strong Love

Ruth

We love because he first loved us.

—1 John 4:19

One thing I tell my children often is this: "I will always love you. Nothing you ever do will make me stop loving you."

Every single time I whisper this simple phrase, I can't help but recall God's unending pursuit of love in my own life. I'm thankful that God did not give up on me. I didn't obey at His first request, but God patiently pursued me, and His unconditional love eventually overcame me.

What drew me to God was not rules, but His gracious invitation for a relationship. It was His love that drew me to love Him. I knew I had fallen short and broken His law. Nobody needed to tell me I wasn't perfect. I needed forgiveness, and I found it when I least deserved it.

The gospel informs us that our acceptance by God as His daughters is based on Jesus' performance, not our own. It's in the context of this loving relationship that we desire to live in obedience: "We love because he first loved us." He took the first step. Our obedience is a response to His love.

This is precisely why our children need to be reminded of our unconditional love for them. They need first and foremost a relationship and not just a list of dos and don'ts. Rules may change behavior, but they cannot change the heart. Our children need us to pursue them patiently even when they don't deserve it as our Father does with us.

We need to be willing to set aside the distractions and the next task because reaching our children's hearts requires our attention. Love slows down and listens.

Listen to your children's hearts. Listen to their fears. Listen to their dreams. Listen to their concerns. Love encourages. It spurs children on without squashing them in the process. Love inspires, casting a vision for doing better.

God's love motivates our obedience to love Him back. Instead of harsh discipline that breaks the spirit, let's remember how our Father lovingly corrects us and reminds us of His unconditional love. Let us do the same for those He has entrusted to us.

Father, thank You for the way You have loved me. Thank You for pursuing me, being patient with me, listening to me, and encouraging me. Most of all, thank You for the grace poured out toward me in Christ. Help me to love my children the way You love me. In Jesus' name, Amen.

- How would you describe God's love for you?
- Do you struggle to show that kind of love to your children? Why?
- In what ways do you most need to express love to your children right now?

The Joneses Are Overrated

Karen

I have learned to be content in whatever circumstances I am. I know both how to have a little, and I know how to have a lot. In any and all circumstances I have learned the secret of being content—whether well fed or hungry, whether in abundance or in need. I am able to do all things through Him who strengthens me.

—PHILIPPIANS 4:11–13 HCSB

Psst . . . I have a little secret.

The Joneses are overrated.

Oh, I know we'd never think that from the way the Joneses appear, but they are not all they're cracked up to be.

In my mom's day, you only saw the Joneses a few times a week. Maybe you bumped into them on your way into church or perhaps at the PTA meeting—you know, as you were getting into your dented gray minivan while they were piling happily into their new spit-shined red Chevrolet.

Now the Joneses perpetually parade in front of our eyes nearly twenty-four hours a day. Where?

On our computer news feeds. And smartphones. On Twitter and Facebook, Pinterest and Periscope, Tumblr and Instagram. The "Look at me!" Joneses and all their profile-picture-perfect lives can tempt us to become jealous and discontent.

One day an online friend posted: "Fettuccini Alfredo, fresh beans from the garden, and my famous raspberry cheesecake. It's what's for dinner!"

A second friend's status read: "Woo-hoo! Paid off the mortgage. We're now debt-free!" And still another, "Our Ethan got student of the month!"

All of this took place while I was ordering pizza (for the second time that week!), piecing together the mortgage payment, and answering a call from the middle school vice-principal's office where my son sat, busted for an inappropriate prank.

Yes, the Joneses invade our homes and our thoughts several times a day through social media and the Internet, robbing us of contentment.

In a letter to the believers in Philippi, the apostle Paul penned Philippians 4:11–13, which says, "For I have learned to be content in whatever circumstances I am" (HCSB). The Greek word rendered "content" in this verse denotes more than just a throwing up of arms in reluctant acceptance. At its hub, it means "to be satisfied to the point where I am no longer disturbed or disquieted."

God has already prepared a place of contentment for us when the car breaks down, the bills are hard to pay, and "our Ethan" acts out . . . again. We find that place when we take our eyes off of our situation—and off of the screen—and fix them solely on God.

To truly embrace our circumstances, we must decide to stop pleading, "God, get me out of here!" and learn to humbly ask instead, "Lord, why have You brought me here? What are You trying to reveal to me that I would never discover if You were to suddenly pluck me out of this situation?"

We can only do this when we stop looking at the Joneses and turn our eyes to Jesus Christ, who gives us strength.

Dear Lord, forgive me for looking around and comparing myself or my circumstances to others. May I look only to You for contentment and peace. In Jesus' name, Amen.

- When you look at what others post on social media, do you struggle with being content with your own life? Why or why not?
- How can asking yourself, *Lord, why have You brought me here? What are You trying to reveal to me that I would never discover if You were to suddenly pluck me out of this situation?* help you to battle discontentment?

A Place of Peace

Ruth

"Blessed are the peacemakers, for they will be called children of God."

—Matthew 5:9

I have four children ages six, eight, eleven, and thirteen years old, so sometimes it seems less than peaceful in my home. Every single day I scramble to spend time mothering my children, doing three to five loads of laundry, helping with schoolwork, cleaning, cooking, and balancing all of the activities we're involved in. It seems we have just cleaned up from breakfast, and it's already time to have lunch. Two minutes later (or so it seems) we're thanking God for dinner.

Managing a household can be overwhelming, and it sure doesn't seem peaceful to me. But Matthew 5:9 says, "Blessed are the peacemakers." When I read those words, I'm reminded that I'm called to be an *instrument* of God's peace everywhere, including in my home.

But there's one problem—and that problem seems to be me. I often wonder, *Am I the one who creates most of the chaos that happens in our day-to-day lives?* We are called to be instruments of peace, but can't we just as easily be instruments of chaos? Am I so focused on my own agenda at times that I can't focus on what really matters?

Ouch. Those questions hit too close to home for me.

As a mother, I'm an instrument of peace at home with my family. God wants to use me to bring peace to my household and into my children's lives. Oh, yes, it can be really hard! But by living intentionally, keeping the most important things at the forefront, I find my days look and feel drastically different.

When I prepare for the day by spending time with God, studying His Word, and praying, I am at peace. Ultimately, without God, we will not have peace.

When I'm nurturing the relationship I have with my husband, I am at peace. Our babes are watching and following our relational lead. If we love each other well, we will bring an atmosphere of peace to our home.

When I'm intentional with my children, I am at peace. We are prone to distraction, but our children need our attention. They need us to squeeze them, encourage them, teach them, laugh with them, read to them, and pray with them. We create a sense of peace when we engage wholeheartedly with our children.

God wants to use us to be instruments of peace in our homes. Will you bring peace to your home today?

Jesus, You are the Prince of Peace. Come and make Your presence known in my home. Quiet my soul, right now, in this place. Reign in my heart and in my home so that this place can be defined by peace. In Jesus' name, Amen.

- What is creating chaos in your home right now?
- What can you start—or stop—doing today to bring more peace into your home?

____

____

____

____

What's in Your Hand?

Karen

"A new command I give you: Love one another. As I have loved you, so you must love one another. By this everyone will know that you are my disciples, if you love one another."

—John 13:34–35

I have a lot of talented friends. Some are crafty and can whip up a festive wreath for the front door or sew a pair of curtains that look like they are from a high-end store. I, on the other hand, don't have one drop of crafter's blood in my veins. My children know better than to ask me to sew a patch on their uniforms. I send them to their dad! If it were left up to me, I would use a hot glue gun. (Been there. Bonded that!)

Other friends I know are skilled at gardening. Their corn, peas, and zucchini burst forth from their meticulously weeded gardens. They have an abundance of healthy produce they can feed to their families. Though I do okay with flowers, herbs, and a tomato plant or two, having a vast vegetable garden to tend has never been my strong suit. So I admire those who take on such an enormous task.

Other friends are renowned for other skills. They may have keen eyes for decorating. Or they are talented with a paintbrush. Maybe they can even repair their own vehicle. So many various talents from so many women I know.

My skills lie in two areas—the kitchen and the pen. I love to cook and I love to write. So for me, I find it easy and enjoyable to bake up a batch of homemade granola bars or to craft a poem for a friend's birthday.

We've all been blessed with unique skills and talents that serve as our signature way to create. But are these talents, hobbies, and abilities just for our own use? Could they serve a greater purpose? Yes! They can all be ways to participate in obeying Jesus' command to us in John 13:34–35. They can be tools for loving others. It all starts with a simple question: what's in your hand?

A garden trowel? What if you showed some love by taking some of your fresh veggies to your neighbors and told them how glad you are that they dwell nearby?

A wooden spoon? Maybe mix up a batch of your famous chocolate chip cookies and give them to your mail carrier as thanks for his or her faithful work.

A paintbrush? Can you paint a picture for a shut-in? Or help paint a dorm room for a new college student? Both would be helpful ways to lighten their loads and lift their spirits.

Loving others doesn't have to be hard work. Simple gestures can have powerful results. May you find natural ways to weave loving others into your busy days by using what is already in your hand.

Father, thank You for the skills, talents, and passions You have given me. Help me to recognize that they are not for me alone. Give me practical and creative ways to love others with what is already in my hand. In Jesus' name, Amen.

- How do you answer the question, "What is in your hand?"
- Brainstorm a few ways to share your unique talents with others

Ask God to bring someone to mind who would be encouraged if she were to receive what you have to give.

What My Thoughts Tell Me

Ruth

Do not conform to the pattern of this world, but be transformed by the renewing of your mind.

—Romans 12:2

Do you ever talk to yourself? Or let me put it another way: Do your thoughts ever talk to you? Thinking is powerful. Our thoughts have a way of snowballing. What starts out as an innocent and random thought can begin to gain momentum if we aren't careful.

Take, for example, the simple thought *I'm failing*. Has that thought ever popped into your head? Maybe you're busy responding to e-mails, or you have just walked through the door from work, or perhaps you have finally tucked the kiddos in to bed. And out of nowhere, as clear as day, you hear these words come to mind: *I'm failing. I'm not good at this. There are better moms out there than me. My kids deserve better.*

The momentum begins to grow. You are not only thinking it; you are beginning to believe it.

The words that appeared out of nowhere found in your mind fertile soil to plant seeds of doubt. And so, pretty soon, the thinking leads to feeling. Not only have you thought you are a failure; you begin to feel like a failure. We all know that once you think, then feel, it isn't too long before you start to act as if those thoughts are true. You become defeated.

Replace the words and thoughts with countless others. They all work the same, don't they? They speak *to* us and *at* us. Thinking is powerful—for good and for bad.

Jesus called the enemy the "father of lies." Oddly enough, the thoughts and words of lies, condemnation, and doubt can sometimes be easier to hear than God's words.

I think this is why the apostle Paul encouraged us, with great urgency and consistency, to renew our minds with the truth of Scripture. We have to get God's Word in us so it shapes and guides our thoughts. We have to read it, meditate on it, and let it do its work in us so that our thinking leads us in the way that is life and truth.

We need to be transformed. Changed. Made new. And this, too, is a work of the Holy Spirit through God's Word. Be careful of being conformed to those thoughts that do not belong to the Father—thoughts and words that are not His. He speaks life and truth.

Let God's words in Scripture renew your mind that you might be transformed into the image of Christ.

Father, give me wisdom to discern between Your voice and the voice of the enemy. I ask You to renew me through Your life-giving Word that is truth. Let it sink deep into my heart and mind so that it will transform me into the likeness of Your Son. In Jesus' name, Amen.

- What do you tell yourself most often?
- In what ways have you let this type of thinking defeat you?
- What recurrent thoughts do you need the truth of God's Word to transform right now?

Benedictions

Karen

*Whoever looks intently into the perfect law that gives freedom,
and continues in it—not forgetting what they have heard,
but doing it—they will be blessed in what they do.*

—James 1:25

Are there any parts of motherhood you feel you need to "suffer through"? Late-night feedings, odious diaper changes, and shrill cries may be taxing, even tiresome, but they are not suffering. These are doses of miracle soul-grow. The unattractive aspects of motherhood are opportunities for us to hear benedictions from the Lord.

The word *benediction* originates from two different Latin words, *bene* meaning "well" and *dicere* meaning "say." In our language, the word is used to describe a spoken blessing. Many times in a traditional religious ceremony, a benediction is spoken at the end of the sermon as a blessing to the congregation and a charge to go forth, to put action to the teaching.

We moms can see the diapers, messes, and sleep deprivation as chances for us to hear a benediction. Why? Because these tasks of motherhood challenge us to take what we learn from the Bible and put it into practice. In the afternoon we can't forget what God told us in the morning.

James 1:25 says, "Whoever looks intently into the perfect law that gives freedom, and continues in it—not forgetting what they have heard, but doing it—they will be blessed in what they do."

We will be blessed in what we do! Not blessed long after the fact or blessed only if someone else notices. No, we can be blessed in the act of service itself! As we vacuum, as we do the laundry, as we clean up the spills, we can be blessed right there in the center of it.

In every mom's life there are challenges and suffering. Challenges are those day-to-day duties that are sometimes punctuated by difficult personalities or situational strife. Suffering happens when we encounter death, persecution for our faith, tragedy, and other acute pains.

Our service to the Lord is valuable training as we seek to become more like Christ. As we practice listening for the benediction, let's get used to recognizing the blessing.

You are cordially invited to cease viewing your motherhood services as "suffering through" but as opportunities to hear God "speaking well" (*benedicere*) to you. Mute the frustration. Press pause. Tune your ear to the benediction.

Dear heavenly Father, help me listen to the blessings that are hidden within each bump in the road. Prepare me to accept small adversities now so I can become a woman who truly praises You in all circumstances. In Jesus' name, Amen.

- How does knowing the original meaning of *benediction* affect your view of mothering?
- How can you approach your tasks and care for your children differently now that you know this?

Parenting Together

Ruth

What causes fights and quarrels among you? Don't they come from your desires that battle within you?

—James 4:1

Though my husband and I were sitting close to each other, we were barely communicating. It wasn't because we were having a fight or didn't want to talk. We were grabbing lunch after church at one of our favorite local restaurants. The diner was busy enough, but our conversation as a family was even livelier! With four kids around the table, there was a lot of chatter and catching up to do.

If you've been married with kids for any length of time, then you know how hard it is to finish a conversation, hold a thought, or maintain order without turning into Sergeant No Fun.

For all the joy that kids bring into a marriage, they can also cause a whiplash effect for a husband and a wife—especially when it comes to parenting. As you probably already know, sometimes our parenting preferences and objectives are at odds with our other half!

Our parenting styles, preferences, and expectations can be different from those of our spouse. If we're not careful, parenting can pull us apart. That's why I love the reminder in James 4:1. It gives us a simple yet profound reason for why we have conflict: most often it comes down to what I want versus what my husband wants.

"What causes fights and quarrels among you? Don't they come from your desires that battle within you?"

This short verse reminds us that we all have desires, but even more important to understand, we have fallen desires. By fallen, I mean desires that have (and often do) come under the influence of our sinfulness. Our sinful desires often lead to disagreements. This is true in every relationship—even in the partnership as parents.

As parents and as spouses, my husband and I may have desires and expectations that are at odds. Likewise, we can have competing desires that are outside of what God wants. Our sin not only separates us from God, but it can also separate us from each other.

Are you and your husband on the same page? Do you have conflicting ideas about parenting? I'm convinced that so many conflicts in marriage, could easily be resolved with open conversation.

Want to get beyond the conflict? Start communicating with your husband today, but do it with humility and grace.

Father, thank You for the gift of our children. Help my husband and me to parent together. Give us honesty, clarity, and humility with each other. In Jesus' name, Amen.

- About what do you and your spouse most often agree? Disagree?
- If you could change one or two things about how you and your spouse parent together, what would they be?

We *Have* To or We *Get* To?

Karen

Whatever you do, do it enthusiastically, as something done for the Lord and not for men, knowing that you will receive the reward of an inheritance from the Lord. You serve the Lord Christ.

—Colossians 3:23–24 HCSB

My life as a wife, mom, worker, daughter, neighbor, church member, and friend brings me much delight. However, my life also brings me lots of to-dos. Purchases to make. Closets to organize. Paperwork to complete. Phone calls to return. Research to be done. Pots and pans to scrub. Kids to shuttle. Parents to check on. And on and on it goes.

Sometimes when I get my list all scrawled out on paper, my mind starts looping the "poor me" soundtrack that results from just looking at my list.

Poor me . . . I have to mop the floors.

Poor me . . . I have paperwork to finish.

Poor me . . . I have to drive to get groceries.

Poor me . . . I have to take my son to practice.

Poor me . . . I have to work on the computer for a few hours to finish this project.

Poor, poor, pitiful me!

Colossians 3:23–24 addresses this "poor me" mentality by giving us a fresh perspective as we go about our work: "Whatever you do, do it enthusiastically, as something done for the Lord and not for men" (HCSB). Three words jump up at me as I stop and ponder this verse:

1. *Whatever*: Not just the tasks I enjoy, or the work that brings me recognition, or the duties that I happen to find fun, but *whatever* I do is to be done . . .

2. *Enthusiastically*: This word is defined as "done lively and with great interest; wholeheartedly, sincerely, energetically and earnestly." Hmmm . . . I'm not so sure that describes my attitude as I tackle the "whatevers" on my to-do list. How about you?

3. *Lord*: It is the Lord Himself we serve as we enthusiastically check off our "whatevers." Not a husband. Or kids. Not a boss or the committee chairperson. We are serving Jesus Christ Himself as we work.

How about we hit the restart button when it comes to our tasks? Let's stop pouting. Rather, let's reframe our attitudes Colossians 3:23-style.

I don't *have* to clean my house. I *get* to clean my house—because I have a place to call my own, while many are homeless or displaced. And I'm serving the Lord Jesus as I clean.

I don't *have* to fill out this team permission slip. I *get* to fill it out—because my child is healthy enough for physical activity. And I'm serving the Lord Jesus as I write.

I don't *have* to drive to get groceries. I *get* to do this errand—because we have enough money to purchase provisions and we own a car, so I don't have to walk. And I'm serving the Lord Jesus as I shop.

We don't *have* to. We *get* to. And thanks be to God that we do.

Father, thank You for all the to-dos on my list. Help me always remember that I'm working for You. In Jesus' name, Amen.

- Name one "have to" item that's on your to-do list today. How could you turn your thoughts about this task into a thankful "I get to" statement instead?

More Than a Mom

Ruth

You died, and your life is now hidden with Christ in God. When Christ, who is your life, appears, then you also will appear with him in glory.

—Colossians 3:3–4

When kids come along, it's easy to get wrapped up in them. And by "wrapped up," I mean your world begins to revolve around them.

To some degree, this is absolutely necessary. Kids need our time, love, affection, help, and support. They are dependent on us for a reason.

But I'm talking more about identity. Who are you? I mean, who are you really? Do you find your identity in being a mom?

People base their sense of worth, lives, callings, and joy on all sorts of things. We might find our identity in what we do, both in our successes or our failures. We can form an identity based on our possessions. We may think what we own defines who we are. And this is why motherhood can be tricky.

Motherhood is a noble and sacred calling. But motherhood can't be the primary source of our identity. We are more than moms. That's not to diminish our role as moms. But it *is* to remind us of our core identity in Christ, as His followers.

The apostle Paul said our life is "hidden with Christ." In Christ, we are His daughters. This identity shapes our calling and how we pursue motherhood. Our identity in Christ is what lays a solid foundation for all that we do—in motherhood, ministry, the workplace, and more.

What is God calling you to do? Do you struggle, thinking that motherhood has to stand in the way of what God is leading you to do? You are a mom, and motherhood is a calling. But are there other dreams and desires that God has put on your heart to pursue?

Your dreams might include starting a blog, writing a book, starting a ministry at your church, or volunteering in a community organization. God has gifted you and wired you to make a difference in the lives of others. Being a mom doesn't mean you can't pursue God's calling to serve Him in other ways.

Start dreaming. Pray hard. And if God is calling you, don't be afraid to take a step of faith.

Father, what is it You are calling me to do for You? I love being a mom. But are there other areas that You would lead me toward to make an impact for Your kingdom? Help me to remember that my identity is first and foremost in You. In Jesus' name, Amen.

- Do you ever feel like there are dreams or desires God has placed on your heart to pursue? What are they?
- What are the biggest obstacles standing in the way of your pursuing God's calling?
- What step of faith will you take to start pursuing what you think God is asking you to do?

From Broken to Boasting

Karen

"So now I give him to the LORD. For his whole life he will be given over to the LORD." And he worshiped the LORD there.

—1 SAMUEL 1:28

Boasting gets a bad rap. At least when I hear the word *boasting*, I think of some championship team gloating over their victory. (This especially makes me fume if my child is on the team that just lost!) But boasting has a place in the life of a mom. Although it's easy and more natural to want to boast about our children, the boasting we should be doing is in the Lord.

Hannah is a woman we meet in the book of 1 Samuel. In chapter 1, the Bible says that she didn't have any children because the Lord had not allowed her to conceive. Because of this, Hannah was deeply hurt. In verse 15 (HCSB), she confessed, "I am a woman with a broken heart." Hannah prayed and made a vow to God that if she were given a son, then she would dedicate him to the Lord for the rest of his life.

God gave Hannah a son whom she named Samuel. After the child was weaned, she took him to the tabernacle so he could serve the Lord: she was keeping her promise. How could she do that? Why would she give up the son whom she had prayed for? I believe we get some answers from Hannah's prayer, recorded just after she left her son.

Hannah prayed, "My heart rejoices in the LORD; my horn is lifted up by the LORD. My mouth boasts over my enemies, because I rejoice in Your salvation. There is no one holy like the LORD. There is no one besides you! And there is no rock like our God" (1 Samuel 2:1–2 HCSB).

Hannah left her son that day and was suddenly in a physically barren place but not a spiritually barren place. Sometimes we find ourselves back where we started but with a whole lot more perspective. When Hannah prayed, there was no rejoicing in Samuel, her son. Instead she rejoiced in the Lord.

Jeremiah 9:23–24 reminds us, "Let not the wise boast of their wisdom or the strong boast of their strength or the rich boast of their riches, but let the one who boasts boast about this: that they have the understanding to know me, that I am the LORD, who exercises kindness, justice and righteousness on earth."

Hannah knew that God is the life-giver and purpose-fulfiller.

Dear heavenly Father, thank You for giving me the gift of motherhood. As You bless my children and allow them to acquire achievements worth bragging about, I pray that I will never boast in them. Let me always boast in You. In Jesus' name, Amen.

- What loss—of something or someone—has brought you closer to God?
- What spiritual growth resulted from your sorrow and grief?

Passing on Your Faith

Ruth

These commands that I give you today are to be on your hearts. Impress them on your children. Talk about them when you sit at home and when you walk along the road, when you lie down and when you get up.

—Deuteronomy 6:6–7

Not long ago my daughter came to my husband and said, "Dad, I'm glad you are a pastor!" When he asked her why, she replied, "Because you teach us the Bible."

Do you ever feel inadequate to lead and guide your children in Bible study? Have you ever felt confused about how or where to begin? If so, you're not alone. The good news is that you don't have to be a Bible scholar, pastor, or trained theologian to pass on to your children your faith in Jesus.

The Lord wants to use you, right where you are, in the middle of the messiness of motherhood. God wants all people to come to a saving knowledge of Jesus, and He desires to work through you.

In a time when many children are growing up in American churches and homes that are less biblically literate than previous generations, it's important as parents that we are intentional about teaching our children the truth of God's Word and guiding them to become rooted in their faith.

There's no perfect formula; the only requirement is a vibrant faith that is alive and growing in you! When God was commanding the Israelites to pass on their faith in Him, He started by saying He wants

His commands to be "on your hearts." Then you can "impress them on your children."

We pass on faith when faith is alive in us. Through conversations at mealtimes, walks in the park, disappointments in school or sports, opening the Bible, prayer, and making decisions. Through teaching, talking, praying, and wrestling with God, our kids get to see invisible faith become visible. What do they see in you? Do they see you living out your faith in Jesus?

Though we know that only Jesus in His grace saves our children, we also know that God has uniquely called the family to help pass along faith to the next generation. What an amazing responsibility and joy to help guide our children toward the Savior!

Father, continue to teach me and guide me. Help me to treasure Your Word in my heart. Renew my faith and help me to pass on faith to my family. May they see You in me and through me. In Jesus' name, Amen.

- How can you as a mom begin taking steps to pass on your faith to your children?
- With whom do you most struggle to talk about your faith in Jesus?
- What are some simple and practical ways to demonstrate your faith in God as you parent?

Canceling the Transaction

Karen

As they make music they will sing, "All my fountains are in you."

—Psalm 87:7

Do you ever wonder how marriage became a complicated equation? Sometimes it seems like your needs plus his schedule equals discontentment. Or his needs plus your exhaustion equals disagreements. Or crying baby plus anything equals frustration.

In marriage, there are also transactions. You give me ________, and I'll give you ________. Give, take. Take, give. We slide into these practices, but it's not the most effective, fulfilling form of doing life together.

I've gotten into this "relationship deposit" mentality, but it leaves me thirsty. I can't help but think of the woman at the well who spoke with Jesus. She had been with five men and was with the sixth.

An interesting thing happened with this woman at the well. Jesus asked her for the very thing that she didn't have. He asked her for water. Well, that's why she was at the well: she needed more. She kept returning to get a drink just like she was trying to fill a heavenly thirst with a human relationship. The men in her life satisfied her only as long as a cool drink did. Jesus came and offered her an eternal spring.

Transactions can only last until someone's account runs dry. One can't give, then the other can't receive, and the relationship falls apart. Jesus invites us to turn away from the transactions and become a spring to our spouse. We do this by recognizing what Psalm 87:7 means when it says, "All my fountains are in you." Our relationship with our spouse no longer has to be a series of give-and-take transactions, but can be like an overflowing spring.

When we abide in Jesus, His living water flows from within us: "Whoever believes in me, as Scripture has said, rivers of living water will flow from within them" (John 7:38). As the rivers flow from within us, not only do we not need a drink, but we have excess life to give to our husband. Excess life means no more empty equations.

Full and free is the marriage in which each member finds his or her fountain in Christ. He is the foundational fountain. As we individually come to the well, our passion-parched hearts become revived with divine romance. Here, we are satisfied.

Dear heavenly Father, thank You for meeting my deepest longings. I am unable to be a spouse without first being a spring of the Living Water that only Your Son can offer. Fill me to overflowing. All my fountains are in You! In Jesus' name, Amen.

- Does your marriage ever feel like a series of give-and-take transactions? Give an example.
- What is your reaction to this statement: "Our relationship with our spouse no longer has to be a series of give-and-take transactions, but an overflowing spring"?

A Work of Art

Ruth

It is by grace you have been saved, through faith—and this is not from yourselves, it is the gift of God—not by works, so that no one can boast. For we are God's handiwork, created in Christ Jesus to do good works, which God prepared in advance for us to do.

—Ephesians 2:8–10

I still have a picture our oldest daughter made for me many years ago. It came at an especially busy and stressful time in my life. And so the thought and creation of her artwork is especially meaningful to this mama!

It's beautiful with all of its colors, shapes, words, and images—made especially for me. To this day, I have it hanging just above my desk where I can see it often. It's a reminder of the love my daughter expressed to me that day.

Did you know God has created you as a piece of art? We are His "handiwork" or "masterpiece." The word in Greek is where we get the word *poem*. The master Artist Himself has crafted each one of us in unique ways. He has made us into something special.

Through Christ, we are His "new creation." Coming to Jesus in faith is just the beginning. It's where God started with us. He has saved us, and is now shaping us, to use us for His good in the world.

This is true as a mom, as a wife, and as a woman. In all of our roles, God has shaped us to do good in the world—to step confidently, equipped by His grace, into His drama.

Imagine if I had failed to see the beauty of the artwork my daughter gave me that day. What if I had dismissed it, paid little attention to it, or simply discarded it?

You are God's work of art, and He continues to shape you into the Christlike person He created you to be. You are a beautiful, powerful piece of art in the hands of the master Artist. The plans He has prepared are not yet finished. So walk in His love. Enter the story of His redeeming grace. Wherever God has you, do good for His glory!

Lord, I want to be molded and shaped into who You want me to be. Help me to remember that You have uniquely made me. You are not changing me just for my own good, but for the good of the world—where You are at work. Give me strength to do what You have created me to do. In Jesus' name, Amen.

- In what ways has God uniquely created you?
- In what ways can God use your past experiences (good and bad) for good in His story?
- Do you struggle to believe you are really God's "handiwork"? If so, why do you think that is?

Break the Yoke

Karen

"Is not this the kind of fasting I have chosen: to loose the chains of injustice and untie the cords of the yoke, to set the oppressed free and break every yoke? Is it not to share your food with the hungry and to provide the poor wanderer with shelter—when you see the naked, to clothe them, and not to turn away from your own flesh and blood?"

—Isaiah 58:6–7

Saturday-morning breakfasts are quite the production around our house. My kids love my homemade whole-grain oatmeal waffles. Grinding the wheat and mixing up the batter isn't simple, but it produces delicious results. We bake our bacon in the oven, making it crispy and avoiding a greasy mess. But most importantly, when frying up eggs, I'm careful to take instructions from my kids: "Mom, don't break the yolk!" they plead. Having an egg sunny-side up with an unbroken yolk puts the finishing touch on their special meal.

There's another type of yoke—same pronunciation, different spelling—that we *are* encouraged to break. In the pages of Scripture, Isaiah recorded for us God's desire to "loose the chains of injustice and untie the cords of the yoke, to set the oppressed free and break every yoke" (Isaiah 58:6). This statement comes in the middle of a passage regarding fasting. Fasting is denying ourselves food—or just certain foods or even certain activities—for a time in order to focus on spiritual things and really hear from God. Yet in the book of Isaiah, God reprimanded the people for their fasting because they were doing it only for themselves—to get something from God. It's then that we are given a description of the type of fasting God desires: it breaks yokes and frees those who are imprisoned.

Today we encounter many who are imprisoned. Oh, we may not know these people personally, but we hear about them and read about them. Women caught in the sex trafficking industry. Those addicted to drugs or alcohol. Minority groups who are oppressed and forgotten. Victims of domestic violence. Those who find themselves caught in the crossfire of a broken home.

As moms, we can not only help to break the yokes of those in bondage to such things; we also can model for our kids how to do the same. By fasting from spending time or money on ourselves, we can free up time and resources to serve and give locally and globally. We can search for organizations and ministries that are in need of help, giving of our time and resources. Others can use our financial help. We as adults can give—and offer opportunity for our kids to part with some of their money too. They can perform extra chores around the house and donate the money they earn.

When we make activities such as these our aim, our families can have a new cry: "Break the yoke!"

Father, allow me to be a yoke-breaker, helping to free those who are imprisoned so they can find the freedom You offer. In Jesus' name, Amen.

→ When, if ever, has your family helped those who are financially disadvantaged or imprisoned by destructive habits or practices? Describe the impact the experience had on your family.

- At what local organizations could your family serve? Reach out to one this week and see how your family can help.

Finding Solitude

Ruth

After he had dismissed them, he went up on a mountainside by himself to pray. Later that night, he was there alone.

—Matthew 14:23

I had just sat down on the couch. Finally! The day was over. I popped open my laptop to check a few e-mails and read the news. The kids were in bed. Silence.

And then my alone time was over.

"Mom? Mom? Mom, I'm thirsty!" My youngest daughter's voice pierced my solitude. My alone time was over before it started!

Motherhood is demanding, isn't it? Oftentimes our day begins with a little one pulling at us, anxious to wake up and start the day. Even nights aren't sacred or off limits with kids.

A nightmare startles your son or daughter awake.

The flu hits.

Someone wets the bed.

Motherhood is anything but easy. And it's far from quiet. All of the demands can be draining. What mom hasn't wanted to lock herself in the bathroom for a few minutes of peace and quiet?!

You should take comfort in knowing that even Jesus, God in the flesh, needed solitude. He, too, knew the busyness of a life in demand. People were always pulling and tugging at Him. The needs were endless. And so He routinely withdrew to "lonely places" (Luke 5:16). He got away.

Slowed down. In all of the giving, He got away to be fed by His Father. Jesus knew and practiced the discipline of solitude.

Before He started His public ministry, He spent forty days in the wilderness (Matthew 4:1–11). Before making important decisions, like choosing the twelve disciples, He spent time alone (Luke 6:12; Mark 1:35). After some of His miracles, He found solitude (Matthew 14:23; Luke 5:16). And, of course, just before Jesus would go to the cross for our sins, He spent some time alone with His heavenly Father (Matthew 26:36–46).

Are you feeling worn-out right now? There's no guilt in getting away. Solitude is a gift God gives us so we can recharge and refill. If we don't spend time away and time alone, the self-neglect can be dangerous. One of the greatest things you can do for your own soul is find solitude.

Father, give me time today to be alone with You. Give me the wisdom to carve out space and time to stop. Help me to push pause and be quiet. Refresh me today. Renew my strength. Pour into me so that I can pour out to my family. In Jesus' name, Amen.

- Do you ever feel guilty for wanting some alone time? Why?
- Where in your schedule will you carve out solitude this week? Even ten minutes count.
- Jesus was purposeful about His solitude. What can you do during your times of solitude to truly recharge?

Stretching for the Savior

Karen

God did this so that they would seek him and perhaps reach out for him and find him, though he is not far from any one of us.

—Acts 17:27

Motherhood stretches me. Does it stretch you too? Many times the demands of being a mom pull me to places I don't want to go.

I might not want to cook dinner. I'd rather order in. I didn't want to get drawn into volunteering each week at the elementary school. I'd rather go shopping. I might've felt yanked into having my daughter's friends over for a slumber party. I'd prefer the house to be quiet. Perhaps I was tugged on to play tag outside when I really just needed a nap. Getting pulled around strains our muscles, tendons, and spirit. This isn't the kind of stretching we need.

The difference between pulling and stretching is the difference between soreness and sanity. Pulling implies resistance; stretching is reaching with desire. Usually a pull takes effort against something. Stretching is effort toward something. Demands pull, but Christ stretches.

So many times I get pulled by my own desire to succeed. I have goals in mind for various mothering pursuits, only to find my labor wearing me out before ever actually accomplish anything. How long until I realize that I cannot stretch to win? I must stretch for the Living Water. Jeremiah 17:8 gently encourages us, "They will be like a tree planted by the water that sends out its roots by the stream. It does not fear when heat comes; its leaves are always green. It has no worries in a year of drought and never fails to bear fruit."

When we let go of all the pulls of being a mom and start stretching for our Savior, we will have all we need. All the deep places within us will be satisfied.

Motherhood is a stretching experience, no doubt about it. The question is, what are we reaching for? God longs for us to "seek him and perhaps reach out for him and find him, though he is not far from any of us."

Let us reach out to Him. He is not far. May our spirit be not strained but satisfied when all our efforts stretch toward the Savior.

Dear heavenly Father, allow me to let go of goal-centered demands that pull me in a direction apart from Christ. Don't let me get wrapped up in the pressure to do certain things. Let me instead stretch toward You. In Jesus' name, Amen.

- In what area of life have you been pulling instead of stretching? What is it?
- How does the definition of these two words help to realign your thinking: "Pulling implies resistance; stretching is reaching with desire"?

Lead by Example

Ruth

Wives, in the same way submit yourselves to your own husbands so that, if any of them do not believe the word, they may be won over without words by the behavior of their wives, when they see the purity and reverence of your lives.

—1 PETER 3:1–2

When Peter wrote these words, he was addressing what Jesus said would happen: some households would be divided over Him (Luke 12:51–53). Faith can bring a couple together, but faith can also drive a couple apart, leading to marital strain, conflict, and even separation.

This is what was happening in the early church when Peter wrote to encourage wives to keep pressing on even if their husbands weren't yet followers of Jesus. It seems that there were some women who had come to faith in Jesus while their husbands had not. And as a result, they were struggling with how to overcome the challenges faced in a split household. What should they do? How were they to balance following Christ and, at the same time, honoring their husbands?

These wives were also wrestling with the temptation to grow discouraged, lose heart, become overzealous in attempting to change their husband's heart, or even stop trying all together. Maybe you are in this place right now. Or maybe your husband is a Christian, but there's still distance between the two of you.

Peter reminded us of an important truth: our lives are the greatest testimony to the gospel. Let husbands be "won over without words by the behavior of their wives." There is a time to speak, a time to bring truth to a conversation, and a time to verbally communicate the good news. But the way we live our lives must be the greatest witness.

We must be respectful, pure, honoring, loving, and gentle. Nobody gets argued into the kingdom. I love this fact because it reminds me that ultimately a changed heart is the work of God. Oh, so many times we try to take matters into our hands. But we can't miss this lesson: we are just instruments, vessels used by God. His love and truth work in us and through us to impact the hearts of those around us.

So if you are in this place, don't give up. Don't lose heart. Trust that God can and will work through you to reach your husband's heart. Let your life be your greatest testimony.

Father, I present myself to You. I want to be a living example of Your grace and truth. I know I can't change my husband's heart. Only You can do that. But use me as a testimony to Your grace. In Jesus' name, Amen.

- If you are in this situation, do you wrestle with walking away, giving up, losing heart, or trying to control?
- Why is it so difficult to trust God to change someone else's heart?
- In what ways can you let your life be the greatest testament to the good news?

From an Eye Roll to an "I Will"

Karen

She sets about her work vigorously; her arms are strong for her tasks.

—Proverbs 31:17

"Don't you roll your eyes at me, young lady," my mama chided. "Just get in there and pick it up, please."

I was in middle school, and "it" was my messy room. After asking me more than a few times to tidy up my little space, Mom was tired of my shenanigans. I would pretend I didn't hear her. Or get busy doing something else—outside, where she couldn't see me. Or I would revert to the old teenage eye roll, the trick I now employed.

But it was no use. If I wanted to hang out at the mall with my friends, attend the school dance, or participate in another such social gathering, I had to tackle "it." And so I turned on America's Top 40 to try to make the task a bit more pleasant and busted through the junk and dust so I could win the prize of time with my friends.

As moms, we, too, face unpleasant tasks that must be done. And redone. And redone once more. I'd love to say that I carry out these duties cheerfully and willingly, but—oh, how I hate to admit it—often, while I might not be rolling my eyes on the outside, the attitude of my mind is that of a resistant teen, trying to get out of a tedious chore.

Proverbs 31:17 describes a mom who set about to do her daily work vigorously. *Vigorously* is defined as "energetically," "heartily," or "for all one is worth."

Ahem. That does not always describe how I do my work—especially unpleasant household chores. Often I perform them reluctantly, begrudgingly, mumbling-and-grumbling-under-my-breath-ingly. Mine is more of an interior eye roll that, while not evident on my face, is in plain sight of God.

Perhaps keeping this verse in mind today will help us to go from an eye roll to an "I will."

I will undertake that project I have been procrastinating on, and I will do it with gusto instead of with aggravation.

I will repeat a household routine I've done countless times as a mom, but this time I will crank up some praise music and thank God that I can move freely and vigorously as I work.

I will heartily help a child with homework or a chore and whisper a prayer of thankfulness to God for the honor of being a mom.

I will run errands around town with a spring in my step and happiness in my heart—rather than a grumpy look on my face and resentment—as I remember how blessed I am to live a life that affords me opportunities for such errands.

You in? We can do this! No more resentful eye rolls. Just hearty and vigorous "I wills" instead.

Father God, please forgive me for the times I have spiritually rolled my eyes rather than vigorously tackled my work. May my attitude shift today. In Jesus' name, Amen.

→ Think of one errand, chore, or responsibility that's on your plate today. How can you complete it with vigor rather than reluctance?

Live with Greater Love

Ruth

This is love: not that we loved God, but that he loved us and sent his Son as an atoning sacrifice for our sins. Dear friends, since God so loved us, we also ought to love one another.

—1 John 4:10–11

Have you ever felt like you missed an opportunity to reach out to someone in need?

Not long ago I was at a small gathering with some women I knew and others I didn't know as well. I felt a nudging from God to talk to a particular woman in the group. Unfortunately, I was too distracted to heed what was most certainly the Holy Spirit. I was tired from a long day and didn't feel like exerting an extra ounce of energy to step out of my comfort zone and reach out to this woman. Later when I got home, it bothered me, but I shrugged it off as no big deal.

A week later I found out that this woman was going through a very difficult time after her husband had left her. I felt sick that I had ignored what God had encouraged me to do. I had been too selfish or distracted to talk to her and encourage her. I had missed an opportunity to reach out.

Unfortunately, this has happened to me more than once. I mean, let's be honest, we have a lot on our plates as moms. But I don't want that to be an excuse. We've all been in situations, with one child pulling on our arm and another asking twenty-one questions, where we can barely finish a thought, let alone think about someone else!

But I'm learning from my mistakes. I'm learning to be more mindful of others' needs. I remind myself often that I have no idea what that cashier at the grocery store is going through, what the receptionist at the doctor's office is facing, or how the young lady I pass in the hallway at church is feeling.

I have a full plate for sure, but so do others. I'm trusting God to give me ears to hear His voice and courage to act. I'm praying for the grace to step out and live with greater love. I want to live on mission as a mom, taking advantage of the many opportunities around me each day.

Let me encourage you today. Be mindful of others. Pray in faith. Keep your eyes wide open, and let God continue to soften your heart toward others. You never know how God will use your smile, your kind words, or your prayers to help someone in need.

Father, give me grace when I fall short. Help me to trust in Your resources. But give me eyes to see those around me who are struggling too. I know the weight I often carry, but help me to lighten the load of others through offering Your love, encouragement, and truth. In Jesus' name, Amen.

- When has someone blessed you at a time you needed it most?
- What is the biggest reason you miss opportunities to minister to others?
- Whom is God calling you to encourage? Choose one or two women to reach out to this week.

Which Four Words Will You Say?

Karen

"What are you willing to give me if I deliver him over to you?" So they counted out for him thirty pieces of silver.

—Matthew 26:15

He went away a second time and prayed, "My Father, if it is not possible for this cup to be taken away unless I drink it, may your will be done."

—Matthew 26:42

Do you enjoy planning? Plans are good, except when they start going off course. And that's just the thing: I see it as a plan gone awry instead of as God saying, "I have a different intent for these minutes or hours."

The last time this happened, I didn't react well. No use sugarcoating anything—I acted like a kid who missed a nap and had gotten her iPad taken away. My behavior was unattractive, to say the least. I had gotten up at the crack of coffee beans, written out an orderly schedule for the day, spent time reading my Bible, and was getting ready to pray. About that time, God crashed my plans. It just seemed to me that *if I* put in the time to read my Bible and diligently lay out the day that God should *give me* smooth sailing. I was doing this for Him.

Right? *Wrong.*

The phrase "give me if I" is an ancient siren song. You can trace this expression back to the motives of many an Old Testament heart. Judas, however, is the only one who betrayed Jesus with these self-serving words.

Let's look at the context of how these words spilled from the lips of the one who abandoned our Lord. Matthew 26:14–16 says, "Then one of the Twelve—the one called Judas Iscariot—went to the chief priests and asked, 'What are you willing to give me if I deliver him over to you?' So they counted out for him thirty pieces of silver. From then on Judas watched for an opportunity to hand him over."

We say these words. It may not seem like we say these words, but we do. Every time we choose our plans over God's plans, we are saying, "Give me if I." The course correction for this misguided phrase is the four words Jesus uttered in Matthew 26:42: "Your will be done."

Divine appointments come in all shapes and sizes. A baby waking up early, a husband needing an extra hand, a coworker needing to chat, or the neighbors needing to borrow two eggs—these can seem like interruptions the Lord wasn't supposed to give us because we had done our part. But "give me if I" sounds like *control,* and "your will be done" sounds like *surrender.*

Sister, this mom deal is like a boat launched into choppy waters. There's no smooth sailing. It's better to surrender to God's plan and allow His will to be done than to fight the wind and the waves each step of the way.

Dear heavenly Father, my words are few today: *Your will be done.* In Jesus' name, Amen.

- Be honest. Which of these four-word phrases do you most often find yourself living out: "Give me if I" or "Your will be done"?
- In what specific situation do you feel the need to transition your

perspective from the first phrase to the second? Craft a sentence prayer to God about this important perspective shift.

Putting "Flesh" on God

Ruth

The Word became flesh and made his dwelling among us. We have seen his glory, the glory of the one and only Son, who came from the Father, full of grace and truth.

—John 1:14

Our family loves the zoo, especially the African safari, aquarium, elephants, monkeys, spiders, reptiles, and unusual birds. Okay—we like it all! It's one thing to read about these creatures from distant lands and exotic places, but it's quite another to get up close and personal with wild animals.

What is it that's so fascinating about seeing a tiger in real life? Why do we stand in awe at the enormity of a hippo, giraffe, or elephant?

Coming close and personal after learning from afar changes our perspective. Our storybook tales put on flesh, and finally they are real.

There's a word that's used to describe God coming to us, coming close to us, a word that means "to put on flesh." It is the word *incarnation*. As Christians, we believe the God of heaven—the God of eternity—came to us in and through Jesus. God "put on flesh." He got close to us. That's wild and mysterious for sure, but in Jesus, God became tangible and touchable.

Jesus' disciples (followers) walked with Him, talked with Him, touched Him, ate with Him, and lived in close proximity to Him. In Jesus, people encountered and experienced the one true God whom they'd only had peripheral access to before.

Making God real to our children begins with us as parents. As moms, we are examples for them. Our children are watching and listening. One of the most powerful, life-changing ways for our children to see God as real and alive is for them to see us following Him wholeheartedly—putting on "the flesh of God" as we live according to the Word of God.

We love and serve others.

We treasure Christ and His Word.

We open our home to friends and neighbors.

We seek God's will in prayer.

We sacrificially give of our time, talents, and treasure.

Before we can expect our children to see God as real, we must live out a faith that's real. This doesn't mean that we live a perfect life. None of us is capable of that except Jesus Himself. But if our life is authentic, through the ups and the downs our children see a mom who clings to God more than anything else. As we live out an active and vibrant faith in Jesus, we help the invisible God become visible to our children.

Father, fill me with Your Holy Spirit. Empower me to live according to Your Word. I want my kids to see You through me. Help me to make Your heart, truth, love, and wisdom tangible to them. Work through me today. In Jesus' name, Amen.

- How have the Christlike examples of other people impacted you spiritually?
- In what ways are you struggling to live according to God's Word?
- What is one way you will "put on the flesh of God" and live out His truth today?

All Ya Need Is Love

Karen

Do not merely listen to the word, and so deceive yourselves. Do what it says.

—James 1:22

One of my favorite passages in the Bible is the Love Chapter, 1 Corinthians 13. I remember being challenged to memorize it for an English class in my public high school in the 1980s. Even secular scholars regard this piece of literature as a beautiful work, captivating in its cadence. It's relatively easy to memorize. Living out the words, however, is a whole different story!

Let's pick up the passage in verses 4–8:

> Love is patient, love is kind. It does not envy, it does not boast, it is not proud. It does not dishonor others, it is not self-seeking, it is not easily angered, it keeps no record of wrongs. Love does not delight in evil but rejoices with the truth. It always protects, always trusts, always hopes, always perseveres. Love never fails.

How would you describe your love for others? Are you a patient soul, or do you drum your fingers and tap your toes while you stew and sigh? Is it hard to bring you to a point of anger, or does flying off the handle come much too naturally? Do you keep score with those who have wronged you, ready to dredge up the past to make your point? Do you boast? Got a case of the green envies? Ever been rude to someone?

How will we ever learn to love the way this passage urges us to?

Here's an idea to help you start living with this kind of love. Write out the words of 1 Corinthians 13:4–8; however, wherever the word *love* is used (or its pronoun *it*), leave a blank. Then try over the next week or so to be able to write your name in the blank when you have a chance to exhibit this quality in real life.

Were you patient at the doctor's office today and, instead of grumbling while sitting in the waiting room, you quietly thanked God for the extra time and then used it to pray for others? Write your name on the "_______ is patient" line. Did you and another family member get into a heated discussion and you were tempted to bring up a wrong from the past but, with God-given restraint, held your tongue? Bravo! Write your name on the "_______ keeps no record of wrongs" line. Were you kind to the grumpy cashier instead of returning rudeness with rudeness? Get out that pen and write away!

Be assured that if you take this challenge, God will give you lots of opportunities to practice displaying these wonderful characteristics of love. And you can count on others noticing the change in you as you seek opportunities to demonstrate God's love.

Dear Lord, help me accurately reflect in my actions the love You show me. When it would be easier to live in the flesh, help me instead to walk in the Spirit. In Jesus' name, Amen.

- Of the characteristics of love mentioned in 1 Corinthians 13:4–8, which is the hardest for you to display?
- With whom is it hardest to live out this quality? Why do you think that is?

- In what ways might the suggested activity help you to change this?

____

____

____

____

____

Gather Around the Table

Ruth

When one of those at the table with him heard this, he said to Jesus, "Blessed is the one who will eat at the feast in the kingdom of God."

—Luke 14:15

What do you see when you look at your dinner table? When I look at ours, I see scratches from a toy car our son drove across it. I see specks of paint that invaded cracks before I was fast enough to wipe them up. I see fingerprints, a few dog hairs (ugh!), and some drops of syrup. There are even a few crumbs I must have missed from last night's dinner.

When we first bought our new table a year ago, I thought it would last forever. The one we had gotten rid of was so well worn—a hand-me-down from my in-laws—that we finally had to let it go. This new table quickly took on a few bumps and bruises, not only from the kids, but also from our Labrador retriever, Blue.

A table is meant to be used. And so I have to remind myself that all of the imperfections are signs that it's more than a nice piece of furniture. It tends to be our home base, stacked with school books and mail. It's also the place we eat, but it's far more than that.

For us, the table is a place we gather. It's like a little altar for us: it's a sacred place where no phones or digital devices are allowed. The table is where we talk, dream, discuss God's Word, laugh, and share life together.

When you read the Gospels, you'll notice how often Jesus shared a table with someone—sometimes sinners, and other times, saints.

Nonetheless, the table was a crucial gathering place. And it's also a picture of what's to come. Throughout Scripture, the table, or great banquet, is a picture of what we will enjoy one day in heaven. In that day communion, friendship, and belonging will be eternal. The table, then, is a little slice of heaven, anticipating the joy that will be ours when Christ comes.

So how do you see your table? Does your family regularly gather to eat, talk, dream, and even look forward to the final Gathering around the table? Far more than just furniture, your table is sacred space. So pull up a chair, pour some more coffee, serve a meal, and gather your family!

Father, help our table to be sacred space. Turn our table into a gathering place for our family. Let it be an altar where we gather as a family, not only to be together, but to worship You. In Jesus' name, Amen.

- How do you see your table?
- How often do you and your family gather at your table? What keeps you from gathering as often as you'd like?
- What can you do to transform your table into more than just furniture, being intentional about the sacred space that it is?

I Didn't Sign Up for This

Karen

You intended to harm me, but God intended it all for good.

—GENESIS 50:20 NLT

"I didn't sign up for this!" my friend moaned as we reviewed the printed class schedules we'd just picked up in the school office. While I had gotten all my desired classes, she had been assigned one she had absolutely no interest in taking.

I tried to empathize, but truthfully I felt she was whining about a minor issue. Her life, in my estimation, was fantastic. She came from a well-to-do family. Her parents had been happily married for more than twenty-five years. She had straight teeth and a newer car.

I, on the other hand, came from a family rocked by divorce and financial struggles. I had only one brother with whom I didn't get along very well. My car was old and ugly. My teeth needed braces, but the funds had never been available. Hearing this friend complain about her schedule started my descent into self-pity as I compared my circumstances to hers.

As I thought about the unfairness of my life, I reached the same conclusion she had when she spied that unwanted class: "I didn't sign up for this!" My friend and I both felt stuck.

In Scripture, Joseph also found himself smack-dab in a heap of hassles and difficult situations he never signed up for: his jealous brothers sold him into slavery. He was whisked away to live in a foreign land. He was falsely accused of raping his master's wife even though he tried his best to stay away from her. He even wound up in prison.

These unjust circumstances could have had him complaining, "I didn't sign up for this!" He could have retaliated against those who caused his turmoil. But he didn't. Joseph maintained a God-fearing, God-honoring attitude throughout his ordeals, even as a slave who had no hope of freedom.

At the end of his life, we get a glimpse into Joseph's continual godly behavior. Wise and discerning, he'd risen from slave to governor of Egypt. When his brothers came during a famine to buy grain from the Egyptian authorities, they were shocked to see their younger brother—long thought dead—sitting in a position of power. The brothers feared Joseph would retaliate for the cruel things they had done to him, but Joseph's response? "You intended to harm me, but God intended it all for good" (Genesis 50:20 NLT).

Joseph refused to let life's hard knocks knock him off course or prevent him from living a life that pleased God. He believed in a God who works all things together for good.

Today when I'm tempted to whine as I compare my life with someone else's, I remember Joseph. I want to emulate his attitude, be spiritually free, and walk in the ways of God.

Dear Lord, help me take my eyes off my circumstances
and fix them solely upon You and Your plan so I can find
true spiritual freedom. In Jesus' name, Amen.

- What aspect of your life has you tempted to protest, "But I didn't sign up for this!"?
- How can Joseph's example help you to think differently about your circumstances?

The Real Me

Ruth

Just as he who called you is holy, so be holy in all you do; for it is written: "Be holy, because I am holy."

—1 PETER 1:15–16

My husband and I both love football, but we strongly disagree about musicals. I love them. My husband? Well, not so much! He'd much rather watch players crushing one another to get a ball than listen to a story unfold through song.

I grew up singing, acting, and performing. The stage was a place where stories came alive. These stories became my stories. Different costumes. Different characters. Tragedies. Romance. I loved everything about the stage.

While becoming someone I'm not to play a role on stage is a good thing in theater, it's not so much a good thing in life. If we're honest, all of us can fall into performing for others.

We go to church. Hang out with friends. Attend a Bible study. Upload photos to social media. But who are we really?

Who is the real me? Not the person I pretend to be, want to be, or even think I am. The real me is my character. It's who I'm becoming through the work of the Holy Spirit in me. I am being made new, changed, transformed, and made better because I'm being made into the image of Jesus.

Because I'm fully accepted and loved in Christ, I don't have to pretend. I don't have to hide. I don't have to act. I can freely present my heart to Christ to be changed by His power and through His Word.

It's the real me that's most important. And it's also the real me that most needs to meet with God often. Who we are is more important to God than what we do. I am not my failures. I am not my successes. I am not my past. My sin does not define me. Because of the forgiveness found in Jesus, I can come out of hiding and be honest about who I am, letting God change me into who He wants me to be.

Father, help me to stop pretending. Help me to rest in Your love and approval. I'm giving You my heart to change me into the mom You want me to be. In Jesus' name, Amen.

- In what areas of your life do you most often pretend to be someone else?
- What part of your character needs God's transforming power?
- Why can focusing on who you are instead of what you do help you as a mom?

Leading with a Look

Karen

"I will instruct you and teach you in the way you should go; I will guide you with My eye."

—Psalm 32:8 NKJV

"Look at my eyes." I always seemed to say these words when I was talking to my young kids. Do you? Usually I was trying to instruct them while they were instead fidgeting with a toy or watching their siblings run around. Other times they were looking down. Sometimes I lifted their chin, and sometimes I just asked them to make eye contact with me so I knew they were listening. I wanted them to see me.

I wish I could say that my eyes are always kind, gentle, and soft, but in reality there are times when they're daggers. In the car I can throw a look from the front seat to the back that lets all participants in backseat quarrels know that another word will mean consequences for all. I'm not condoning my behavior—I'm just admitting that the struggle is real.

"The look" doesn't always work because sometimes our kids aren't watching. When my kids aren't watching, I employ different methods of parenting, which include but are not limited to: tearing through the house trying to catch the children, snapping my fingers incessantly to get their attention from across the room, or opening the pantry in order to toss out quick thrills to distract their lips from more yelling. These tactics do not fall into the category of "instructing."

So what's a mom to do?

Show them how to listen with their eyes.

Psalm 32:8–9 says, "I will instruct you and teach you in the way you should go; I will guide you with My eye. Do not be like the horse or like the mule, which have no understanding, which must be harnessed with bit and bridle, else they will not come near you" (NKJV).

God doesn't want to lead us by pulling our chin to look a certain direction. He desires for us, in our own hearts, to want to go a certain way. We know He wants us to go a certain way because we can look in His eyes and see it.

Speaking and listening with our eyes make for more intimate conversations. When we love someone, we can see the words in their eyes before they say them. What if our children were to follow us this way? What if we spoke instruction with a look and they followed because they were watching us?

Better yet, what if we were to follow God this way so our children have an example of what walking with Him looks like?

Better still, what if they learn how to do this in their relationship with God so that they grow up looking the Lord in His eyes, understanding His cues, and discerning His will for them?

Dear heavenly Father, let me intimately know You so I can raise children who fervently follow You. In Jesus' name, Amen.

- On a scale of 1 to 10 (1 being *I don't ever do this* and 10 being *I always do!*), rate how well you listen to God with your eyes, how well you scour His Word and fix your gaze on His face.
- What will you do to raise this number?

Leaving and Cleaving

Ruth

That is why a man leaves his father and mother and is united to his wife, and they become one flesh.

—Genesis 2:24

One of the opening chapters of the Bible describe God's design for marriage. It is a sacred covenant between a man and woman, joined together by God and for God. But the Bible uses two critical words to describe this covenant: *leave* and *cleave.*

Most translations use the word *united,* although some older translations use *cleave.* It means to stick together, be committed, or hold fast to each other. Isn't this what we promise when we walk down the aisle? We are two individuals becoming one. But in order for this one flesh, this unity, this holding fast to work, there must be a leaving behind.

In particular, we are to leave our parents. This certainly doesn't mean we abandon our parents or no longer have a relationship with them. Clearly the Bible teaches that we are to honor our parents whether we are married or unmarried (Exodus 20:12).

But leaving does mean that our marriage relationship should become our most important relationship. It means our spouse becomes our priority. Leaving means working to protect the marriage relationship—even from parents, in-laws, and extended family.

Sometimes a husband or a wife fails to fully leave, and the good intentions, opinions, or even expectations of extended family can come between the couple. It's not always easy to chart a new course, establish boundaries, and begin weaving a new story together—your story.

If you are struggling in this area, be careful of letting even your own family come between you and your spouse. These relationships can be the hardest to balance. Focus on keeping your marriage relationship the priority relationship. Grow in oneness. Cling to each other.

God has joined the two of you together, one man and one woman, for one life. Don't lose sight of weaving your own story as you cleave to each other. God has given marriage as a gift to be enjoyed and to bring life to each spouse.

Father, thank You for the gift of marriage. Thank You for blessing me with a family. Give my husband and me wisdom for keeping our marriage relationship the priority relationship. Help us set boundaries so we can truly cleave to each other. In Jesus' name, Amen.

- When have family members, even those with good intentions, come between you and your husband?
- In your marriage, in what ways has leaving been difficult?
- What are some specific ways you can establish and maintain healthier boundaries with extended family members?

Scurried or Seated?

Karen

She had a sister called Mary, who was seated at the Lord's feet, listening to His word. But Martha was distracted with all her preparations.

—Luke 10:39–40 NASB

I glanced at the clock on the wall. How was it 11:45 a.m. already? I wasn't even halfway through my to-do list for the morning.

My day had started hours earlier when I had bounded out of bed with the goal of checking off a bevy of tasks I'd scrawled on a legal pad. My list included things to cook, calls to make, and errands to run. Now at midday, I still had four or five items left to do and no way to accomplish them before my 1:00 p.m. dental appointment.

My spirit sank. *What's my problem?* I wondered. Did I underestimate how long each task would take? Or did I overestimate my ability to execute them quickly? Maybe it was a little bit of both.

I also hadn't factored in the interruptions. A text from my daughter needing help on a tax form. An e-mail from a friend wanting a recipe because she had company coming over. More distractions and delays.

A little nervous about my dental appointment, I called my friend Mary to ask for prayer. As we talked, I shared the details of my frustrating morning and asked how her day was going. Mary replied that she hadn't completed what she'd hoped to either, concluding, "But I had a good, long time alone with God this morning praying and reading my Bible, which is what I needed most, so it's okay."

My heart sank as I realized my problem: I hadn't taken time for the most important activity of the day; spending time with God hadn't been on my radar. Maybe if I had spent time with Him, I wouldn't have felt so frustrated by my lack of productivity.

Luke 10 tells of another woman who put chores ahead of spending time with Jesus. Martha was busy scurrying to get to the end of her to-do list, but her sister, Mary, chose a different path. She settled herself at Jesus' feet, soaking in His words and His presence.

There's no doubt Martha's sister, Mary, also had things to do. So did my friend Mary. But in the case of each Mary, she chose to do the best thing first: position herself where she could hear from the Lord.

Perhaps today we can set aside our to-do lists until we've followed the example of the Marys. Let's vow to meet with God before we attempt to meet the challenges of the day. Yes, maybe that's the key. Let's stop scurrying and be seated instead. There's always plenty of room at His feet.

Dear Lord, help me to take time today to meet with You before I try to tackle the tasks of the day. Give me the perspective that You are more important than my never-ending to-do list. In Jesus' name, Amen.

- When planning out your daily tasks, how often do you factor in time to meet with Jesus? Why do you think that's the case?
- If you don't regularly do this, what can you do to begin to build this habit into your day?

Spiritual Children

Ruth

To Timothy my true son in the faith: Grace, mercy and peace from God the Father and Christ Jesus our Lord.

—1 Timothy 1:2

"Who wants a Popsicle?" I heard our son yelling to his friends. Almost before he could finish the question, I saw hands go up. *That's a lot of Popsicles,* I thought to myself. With four kids and a house that attracts many others, we go through heaps of food and water!

Our house has an extra lot that's the perfect space for soccer games, whiffle ball, football, and just about any other sport. As a result, our home often becomes a gathering place for the kids in our neighborhood.

And at times it can be hectic. The noise can be a bit loud, according to one of our neighbors. But we love that our kids have friends who come to our house. Because we are moms, our world is full of kids—not only our own, but other people's as well.

When the apostle Paul called young Timothy his "true son" in the faith, he was saying something significant. Paul was saying that in Christ, he had become like a parent to Timothy.

A thought occurred to me one day when I was watching these kids run through our backyard. Many of them come from Christian homes with parents we know and respect. But others come from homes where God's Word isn't taught or lived out. Some of the children we've gotten to know come from broken homes that don't resemble anything like our own.

And so it hit me that day: I can be a spiritual parent to these kids. I may not be their mom, but by God's grace, I can still speak truth and light into their lives. I can use the opportunities I have to show them the love of Christ. We as a family could be an example to them in simple, everyday ways.

Whether we are offering these kids encouraging words, inviting them to church, asking them questions, or having them over for dinner, we as a family can make an impact for Christ.

Think for a moment about the friends your children have. Are there children, other than your own, to whom God is calling you to be a living example of Jesus' love? Who are the boys or girls who need a spiritual parent?

God can use us not only to shape our own children for eternity but also the children outside of our family. You, too, have the opportunity to guide spiritual sons or spiritual daughters toward Jesus.

Father, let me be an example to those who are outside of our family. Help me be a spiritual mom to the children we have contact with so that they might come to know You and love You like we do. Give us opportunities to share who You are and what You have done for us in Christ. In Jesus' name, Amen.

- Who were the most influential adults in your life aside from your parents when you were growing up?
- What kind of lasting impact did those other adults have on you?
- What are ways you can have a Christlike influence on the kids your children are connected to?

But I'd Rather Sleep Than Pray

Karen

Then He came to the disciples and found them sleeping. He asked Peter, "So, couldn't you stay awake with Me one hour? Stay awake and pray, so that you won't enter into temptation. The spirit is willing, but the flesh is weak."

—MATTHEW 26:40–41 HCSB

I was intrigued when I saw a pamphlet titled "How to Spend an Hour in Prayer." I often find it difficult to keep my thoughts from wandering when I pray. They ricochet all over the place as I try to focus. So when I found this nifty little resource, I decided that things were going to change.

One day I settled myself on a park bench, opened my Bible, and began to do what the pamphlet suggested: "First, spend five minutes thanking God for the blessings in your life."

Pretty soon a jogger trotted by. Then two hyper squirrels decided to chase each other up and down a tree and around my bench. I laughed at their antics and lost my train of thought. Even when the animals and humans quieted down, I still had trouble concentrating.

I couldn't focus; I kept thinking of all the things on my to-do list. And I was tired! The thought of chucking my plans and heading home to take a nap seemed like a better idea. So, after about twenty-three minutes, I gave up, packed up, and headed home. My conclusion? I just wasn't cut out to be a prayer warrior. I'd rather sleep.

It seems I'm not alone. The Bible tells us that even Jesus' disciples had a hard time with prayer. They fell asleep when Jesus asked them to stay awake with Him the very night before He was crucified. Jesus verbalized the trouble with our best-intentions-turned-sour when He told His disciples, "The spirit is willing, but the flesh is weak" (HCSB). How true!

My spirit wants to connect and converse with God, but my flesh would rather be getting things done. Or mentally making my grocery list. Or—worst of all—even catching some z's!

In order to see progress in our prayer life, we need to make *prayer* a matter of prayer! No, that isn't a typo. We must pray first—before anything else—that God would help us rein in our wandering thoughts.

We won't turn into prayer warriors overnight. But we'll want desperately for Jesus to meet us in our weakness and teach us to do the hard work of making prayer a priority. He is faithful. We must be too.

Father, forgive me for the times I have let my flesh win when my spirit wanted to pray. May I never cease trying to develop the important habit of spending intimate time with You in prayer. In Jesus' name, Amen.

- What is your biggest distraction during prayer?
- What are some ways to overcome that distraction, enabling you to focus?

Teaching Forgiveness

Ruth

Be kind and compassionate to one another, forgiving each other, just as in Christ God forgave you.

—Ephesians 4:32

"You need to tell your sister you're sorry," I said to our oldest son. We had been in the car for too long. Our kiddos weren't the only ones feeling antsy. I was ready—maybe even more ready than they were—to get to the restaurant. I was starving.

"It's not just what you say; it's how you say it," I continued. This little exercise in conflict resolution was not going well. The kids were tired. I was tired. I was saying all of the right things but feeling uglier and uglier on the inside. And then it happened—a classic meltdown moment. Unfortunately, I was the one having the meltdown! All of the emotion boiled over inside of me. Raising my voice and letting anger get the best of me, I failed at being the peacemaker.

Now I was the one who needed to say, "Please forgive me." And so I did. I had to eat my own words. There in the car, I reminded our kids that their mom isn't perfect either. I'm a sinner who has to look to Jesus—often. I need His grace to cover me when I fall short and to empower me to walk in obedience.

This wasn't the kind of teaching moment I would prefer! I'd much rather tell a story or share a devotional about why forgiveness is necessary instead of being the example. But there was something powerful about that exchange.

My meltdown in the car wasn't the first time I messed up, and it wasn't the last. As moms, we fall short often. Exhaustion and stress can leave us vulnerable to sinning instead of being a shining example to our kids.

And yet even when we fall, God can use those moments, those shortcomings, for something good. Our missteps can be great opportunities for us to lean into Jesus. To trust Him more deeply. To rest once again in His abundant grace. And, in the process, to teach our kids to do the same. When we fall short, they get to see not only our mistakes but also God's favor.

Father, thank You for Your grace when I fall short. In my sin, teach me to treasure You more and more. Thank You for Your forgiveness. Use my failure to teach my kids to trust You, depend on You, and look to You as their Savior. In Jesus' name, Amen.

- When are you most vulnerable to having a meltdown?
- Why do you think it's often so difficult to say, "I'm sorry" or "Please forgive me"?
- It's easy to just want a conflict to be over and the peace and quiet to return. What do you think is the difference between truly teaching how to forgive and simply ending a conflict? Which do you most often do?

Friend or Frenemy?

Karen

Faithful are the wounds of a friend; profuse are the kisses of an enemy.

—Proverbs 27:6 ESV

I'm a sap for words and reading. I adore books—their look, the feel of their pages, and even their smell. Not content to sit still in a waiting room, I'll pick up anything within reach and read it. Why, I still even read cereal boxes at breakfast!

I love to learn new words, thereby increasing my vocabulary. And I'm intrigued by the new words that are added to our language as the years go by.

Every so often, dictionaries must be updated with new words. In fact, *Merriam-Webster* has added more than a hundred entries to the latest edition of its *Collegiate Dictionary*. One of the new words listed in this latest round leapt off the page at me: *frenemy*. It's defined as "one who pretends to be a friend but is actually an enemy."

This era of social-networking sites has given rise to the number of frenemies who come out of the woodwork. I've heard school-aged girls talk about accepting someone as a friend on Facebook, not because they like her and really want to be her friend, but to spy on her and keep up with what's happening in her life—who she likes, where she goes, who she hangs out with.

Even grown women befriend people on these sites just to nose around. In actuality they can't stand some of those they are "friends" with. So the backbiting and tongue-wagging continue even as our posted profile faces smile at each other. False, fake . . . frenemies.

The worst frenemy, however, is the greatest deceiver of all. He promises happiness but delivers sorrow. He tricks and traps and leaves us regretting of our choices. His ways sparkle and glitter and entice. But in the end, they are dark. Like a lion in sheep's clothing, he comes to steal, kill, and destroy. Beware! "Be sober-minded; be watchful. Your adversary the devil prowls around like a roaring lion, seeking someone to devour" (1 Peter 5:8 ESV). Flirting with the devil *never* has a happy ending!

Let's take our new vocabulary word today and vow to be on our toes about frenemies. Let's avoid them and certainly not be a frenemy ourselves. Let's watch out for the biggest one of all—Satan. And may God give us an others-centered love, as only He can give.

Dear Lord, keep me alert for those who do not have my best interests at heart. Send me true friends. Help me be an authentic friend. Keep me from the snares of the greatest frenemy of all. In Jesus' name, Amen.

Our friendships should be pure, honest, and true. As for our enemies, Jesus told us exactly how to respond to them: "But I say to you who hear, Love your enemies, do good to those who hate you, bless those who curse you, pray for those who abuse you" (Luke 6:27–28 ESV). How does this speak to you today?

Is Your Home Fun?

Ruth

The fruit of the Spirit is love, joy, peace, forebearance, kindness, goodness, faithfulness, gentleness and self-control. Against such things there is no law.

—Galatians 5:22–23

"What's wrong, Mom?" my oldest daughter asked. "Nothing," I said. "I'm fine." She wouldn't let it go. And so she asked another question. "Well, then, why do you look so mad?" "Mad?" I asked. "I'm not mad. I'm busy, but I'm not mad!"

Little did I know, I had been wearing a scowl on my face for most of the day. Moving from one task to another, I was oblivious to what my countenance looked like to my kids. After all, I was on a mission! I had work to do! This mama had her game face on! And apparently everyone in the house knew it except me.

Organizing bills.

Putting away dishes.

Feeding the dogs.

Making lunch.

Cleaning up a mess.

Helping with homework.

You know the list, right? As moms, we all know the to-dos are never done. Sometimes more seems to be on the list at the end of the day than when we began. And yet when my daughter caught me with that stern look on my face, it occurred to me that I can't overlook fun in our home.

Now, I'm not suggesting we need to whistle every time we work around the house or smile continuously while we are doing homework with the kids. Let's get real: not everything is fun!

But my daughter's question was a convicting reminder that in all of the seriousness, busyness, and stress of mothering, we can't forget to have fun with our kids. Our children need joy. They need our lightheartedness as much as they need our love. We should never become so busy that we miss time to laugh, slow down and snuggle, get on the floor and wrestle, or just lounge on the couch and tell goofy stories.

We need to slow down enough to make room for fun. At times I will use the phrase "turn that frown upside down" with one of my children. I need to tuck that away and remember that myself!

So let's be honest: Would your kids say your home is fun? How would they describe your mood? Let them see your spontaneous side. Surprise them with a little fun!

Father, fill me with joy. In all of the hard stuff, give me laughter. Fill me with peace. Give me a light heart because I know You and am safe in Your arms. Let my home be a place where true joy is visible and felt by my children. In Jesus' name, Amen.

- If you were to ask your children to describe your home, what one word do you think they would use?
- What is the greatest thief of joy in your home right now?
- What are some ways you can bring more fun into your home?

Minivans of Clay

Karen

We have this treasure in jars of clay to show that this all-surpassing power is from God and not from us.

—2 Corinthians 4:7

I never wanted a minivan. I supposed that if I had to drive one someday, I might die from the ordinariness of it all. I wasn't wishing for a hot rod or pink Cadillac, but when I was younger I just pictured something . . . Well, anything but a minivan.

Having a minivan meant that I had a need for one. Having a need for one meant that I would be a mom. Now, I believed motherhood was going to be awesome, but I had aspired to be a stylish supermom. See, *stylish* and *minivan* just don't go together. Oh, I can laugh so hard at that younger version of myself!

Guess what I learned? *Stylish* and *burp cloths, breastfeeding pads, explosive diapers, children's middle-of-the-night sickness*—they don't go together either. Being a mom is anything but glamorous. It's gritty. It's gum-in-the-hair gooey. It's frantic. And maybe the hardest aspect is that sometimes it's really ordinary and completely commonplace.

How could being a minivan mama draw people to Christ? There's nothing noticeable or flashy about the role. No high-level or visible position. No missionary tales from foreign soil. No gospel crusades on the streets. Nothing extraordinary.

Except . . . *everything* extraordinary.

Flashy on the outside wasn't how Jesus rolled, and flashy on the inside doesn't come from us. We roll in minivans of clay so that God's awesomeness is clearly recognized for what it is: Him and not us.

The Bible says of Jesus, "He grew up before him like a tender shoot, and like a root out of dry ground. He had no beauty or majesty to attract us to him, nothing in his appearance that we should desire him" (Isaiah 53:2). Our Lord wasn't described as flashy. His looks didn't draw attention. He didn't have a regal aura about him. He was ordinary in appearance rather than stylish and stunning.

Outsiders might not be attracted to our snarly, hairy motherhood moments. It's the patience, love, and supernatural something about those clay minivans carrying Jesus-following mamas that will ultimately win people over.

The world doesn't need more bling. It needs more clay.

Dear heavenly Father, let me be humble. I don't need to live a glamorous life; I *get* to live a glorious life—not because of myself, but because of the sparkling riches of Christ in me. Let everyone see nothing noticeable on the outside, but everything magnificent on the inside. May it be clear that this treasure is from *You*. In Jesus' name, Amen.

→ Name one ordinary task as a mom you must complete today. Now, how can you realign your thinking about that task to see it as a glorious offering rather than an unglamorous chore?

Stepping Out in Faith

Ruth

Against all hope, Abraham in hope believed and so became the father of many nations.

—Romans 4:18

Having faith and walking by faith are not the same, are they? Many people might say they "have faith." They believe the right things, which is important—having a mental agreement with the truth. But "walking by faith" is another story. This kind of faith, which is true faith, requires more from us. It requires us to risk, to step out of what we're comfortable with, what we know, and sometimes even what we like. Walking by faith requires action, and sometimes taking action can be dangerous.

The story of Abraham in the Bible is one of my favorites. His story, like mine, is a reminder that God uses imperfect people to accomplish His perfect purposes. God doesn't expect us to be faultless, but He does ask us to walk by faith.

It's what made Abraham leave his hometown, leave behind family, and go. He went where God called him, trusting that God would already be where He was leading him.

"Against all hope," the apostle Paul wrote. In other words, Abraham's walking by faith was met with resistance, real-life obstacles, and seemingly impossible circumstances. What God asked Abraham to do didn't always make sense. But again, almost in defiance of those things, "Abraham in hope believed." He sprang into action. He did it anyway. He walked by faith.

So what about you? What is God asking you to do that will require faith? Maybe it's not leaving your hometown or moving to a foreign place. It might not be physically dangerous. But when was the last time taking a step of faith made you uncomfortable?

God wants us as moms to put our faith into action, trusting Him to be our Provider and Protector. Your step of faith might entail starting a Bible study for moms in the neighborhood or inviting another mom over for coffee. Maybe it's hosting a day at the park for moms you don't know well or who aren't Christians.

Don't let fear keep you from walking by faith! Don't play it safe. Take a step, and when you do, you will find that God is there. Let your obedience be the place where God shows up and does a great work in you and through you.

Father, give me courage. Help me to take a step of faith. I don't want to just *have* faith; I want to *walk* by faith. Give me opportunities. And when they come, give me boldness to obey for Your glory. In Jesus' name, Amen.

- What are your most common fears about walking by faith?
- When have you seen God show up before when you have taken a step of faith?
- What is God calling you to do that you have been pushing aside out of fear?

Making the Resurrection Real

Karen

Great is the Lord*! He is most worthy of praise! No one can measure his greatness. Let each generation tell its children of your mighty acts; let them proclaim your power. I will meditate on your majestic, glorious splendor and your wonderful miracles.*

—Psalm 145:3–5 NLT

The television host leaned over to make sure the microphone was close to the precocious girl's mouth. He'd just asked her, along with a panel of other school-aged children, about the real meaning of Easter. Her classmates' answers ranged from getting candy and trinkets from the Easter Bunny to marking the official beginning of spring.

This youngster seemed to have an answer that was more spiritual and accurate than the others: "Easter is the time when Jesus died on a cross for our sins and got buried in a tomb."

"That's right!" the host responded. "But He didn't stay in the grave, did He, honey? Tell the audience what happened next."

"Oh, that's easy!" she exclaimed. "He rose from the dead and came out of the grave." The host smiled and started to commend the little girl for her correct answer. But before he could, the no longer camera-shy student heartily added, "And each year, if He sees His shadow, there will be six more weeks of winter!"

Holiday traditions can get mixed in with the real essence of holy days, which can be confusing, like when that sweet girl merged Easter with Groundhog Day. As a child, I wondered what Santa caravanning his reindeer through snowstorms had to do with baby Jesus being born in Bethlehem. And I never did figure out why the Easter Bunny brought me chocolate eggs each year. Didn't chickens, not rabbits, lay eggs?

Today's passage from Psalms encourages us to teach our children about God's mighty acts. I can't think of a more powerful act than when God raised His only Son, Jesus, from the dead, making a way for us to gain access to heaven to live with Him for all eternity.

There are many fun, family-bonding traditions to celebrate throughout the year, whether at Easter, Christmas, or even a birthday. With a little thought and planning, we can also work into our celebrations the reminder that the greatest celebration of all is centered on Jesus' resurrection from the grave. It is the meaning of Easter, the fulfillment of Christmas, and the new birth we are all invited to experience.

Let's be intentional about telling of God's mighty act of raising Jesus from the dead to the generations that come after us. Fun traditions are enjoyable and memorable, but the truth of the redemption story is the most wonderful news of all!

Dear Lord, help me to tell of Your wondrous power and mighty acts to those generations that come after me. In Jesus' name, Amen.

- On a scale of 1 to 10 (1 being *never* and 10 being *always*), how intentional are you about bringing Christ and the story of salvation into your celebrations?
- How would you like to see this change in the future of your family celebrations?

Judge Not

Ruth

"Do not judge, or you too will be judged. For in the same way you judge others, you will be judged, and with the measure you use, it will be measured to you."

—MATTHEW 7:1–2

She was struggling to keep her kids under control. With each of her children obviously on the verge of a tantrum, this mom was moving through the grocery store checkout as fast as she could.

One child was reaching for a pack of gum wrapped in shiny purple plastic. Her youngest, visibly upset, was still recovering from a "no" that likely took place somewhere in aisle 17—the toy aisle. The mom was walking on pins and needles.

Watching all of this unfold and wondering what was next, I began to imagine what I would do if I were her.

I would have . . .

She shouldn't . . .

If my son were doing that, I would . . .

Sound familiar? As quickly as I started to put myself in this woman's shoes, imagining the ways I would mother her children better, I realized what I was doing: I was making judgments. Judgments about her kids' behavior, how this mom was trying to discipline her kids, and what she should or shouldn't do. Of course they were unfair judgments. I lacked any real information, understanding of her circumstances, or compassion.

My judgments were also fueled by pride. I hate to admit it, but I was judging her parenting by comparing it to mine—blind to my own many weaknesses and shortcomings! It's so easy to judge, isn't it?

We can judge what other families eat, what they wear, how they discipline, the movies they watch, how they sit in church, how they play with others, and the list goes on. It's not that there aren't right and wrong ways to do things. But we have a tendency to see someone else's sin before we see our own.

Jesus wasn't saying we should never make judgments. But He taught that we need to first look into our own hearts and remove the "plank" from our own eye.

We never know how far someone has come, and we're not always sure what another family is going through. As moms, we need to be careful of thinking that the way we do things is the *only* way to do things. Instead, we need to walk humbly with one another and always extend grace, remembering how much we ourselves are in need of it.

Father, guard my heart against pride. Help me to be humble, gracious, and understanding. Give me eyes to see my own sin and my need for You. Empower me by Your Spirit to take my eyes off of others and keep my eyes on You. In Jesus' name, Amen.

- What prompts you to make judgments about someone else's mothering?
- How has God used motherhood to make you more humble?
- What are some specific ways you can show greater compassion to other moms?

Treasures Among the Trash

Karen

Now you must also rid yourselves of all such things as these: anger, rage, malice, slander, and filthy language from your lips. Do not lie to each other, since you have taken off your old self with its practices and have put on the new self, which is being renewed in knowledge in the image of its Creator.

—COLOSSIANS 3:8–10

My mom was a fanatic about spring-cleaning. Each year in April or May, when the first string of sixty-degree days made its appearance in chilly Michigan, my brother and I would grab our brushes and buckets and help Mom spring-clean the house. She would open the windows to let in the crisp spring air. We washed walls and windows, cleaned carpets and closets. We took down, washed, and re-hung curtains. We beat rugs and straightened shelves, threw away broken toys, and donated too-small clothing.

We even had to de-junk and organize the garage—the most dreaded task. Even though my mom didn't particularly enjoy this yearly routine, in our family, it wasn't optional. She taught us that if we were consistent in keeping up with these nasty chores, they could be tackled before they reached the point of no return. It was hard enough to wash those walls with a year of accumulated residue from our oil-burning furnace on their surface. Just imagine how difficult the job would be after two or three years!

I will be honest and say it that even though I dreaded those few days each year, I also loved the feeling I got when spring-cleaning week was over. The house's surfaces seemed to sparkle. The air smelled lemony fresh. The shelves, closets, and drawers looked neat and tidy.

And, as an added bonus, this spring-cleaning enterprise would often unearth some prized possession that I thought had long been lost. A treasure among the trash. Once it was a favorite Skipper doll. Another year, my bright red Etch A Sketch. Later, a cherished issue of *Tiger Beat* magazine. If I hadn't participated in this annual ritual, I'd never have rediscovered these important items!

Our homes are not the only things in need of a good spring-cleaning. Often our hearts also require some purging. We must be in the habit of looking deep into ourselves to rid our hearts of any thoughts, habits, or feelings that are making us dingy and dull: envy, jealousy, hatred, discontentment, impatience, unkindness, or revenge. Though these reside in our hearts, they often manifest themselves on our tongues.

When we make the effort to bring our hearts to God, asking Him to do what only He can do, He will forgive our sinful attitudes and resulting actions and make our hearts new again. Then maybe we'll be able to unearth some cherished treasures we thought were long lost: love, joy, peace, patience, kindness, goodness, faithfulness, gentleness, and self-control.

Isn't it time you gave your heart a good spring-cleaning?

Dear Lord, forgive me for sometimes paying more attention to cleaning my house than to cleaning my heart. Please rid my heart of anything that is displeasing to You. I give You the bucket and brushes. Make my heart fit for service to the King. In Jesus' name, Amen.

→ What unhealthy emotion are you harboring in your heart today?

→ Now, what could you replace it with instead? Spend a few moments talking to God about this change of heart.

Faith That Waits

Ruth

Blessed is she who has believed that the Lord would fulfill his promises to her!

Luke 1:45

Have you ever experienced a season of waiting? Maybe you have found yourself frustrated, impatient, and even discouraged by the wait. For most of us, waiting isn't easy.

Recently my husband and I experienced a time just like this. For two years we strongly felt God calling us to something else. The problem was, we weren't sure what that "something else" was. We felt a little like Abraham when God said, "Go," and then, "I'll show you where." We were certain that God had us serving at the church where we were for an interim period. And so we prayed and we waited.

The seeking, searching, trusting, and waiting were hard! To be honest, although we felt His nudge, it seemed as if God's answer would never come. Over and over I said to my husband, "I know God has something else for us. We just need to be patient. It's not time yet."

Most of the time, waiting doesn't make sense to us. But God uses such seasons to strengthen our faith. Waiting is not wasting time. God is using the waiting to do something in us before we can do something for Him. God can use the waiting to refine, humble, or shape us for what's next. He's looking for a faith that is willing to wait on His plan and His timing.

I have been reminded of this anew as our strong feeling of "something else" has unfolded. Although we loved the church where we served,

God was calling us to plant a new church. When God impressed this on our hearts, we had no idea what would happen. Like anyone who has ever stepped out in faith, we experienced fear, uncertainty, and plenty of excitement too. God was telling us it was time to go, time to trust Him with the next steps. So we did.

As we announced our decision to leave, we began to see God's gracious hand of provision. Not that there haven't been challenges, but God has proved Himself faithful—we sold our house without ever putting it on the market, He raised up families to go with us, and He provided income we desperately needed. The waiting was over, and God was moving us forward. The waiting was certainly worth it.

As I share this with you, we're still at the beginning of this journey, but one thing I'm certain of is this: God's timing is always perfect, and He's looking for faithful people who will be sensitive to His calling and willing to wait in faith for Him to answer.

Father, teach me to wait on You. Help me not to get out in front of You or lag behind You. During this season, shape me and mold me. Give me a heart that's willing to wait on You and courageous enough to go when You call. In Jesus' name, Amen.

- In what ways has God used waiting to shape you?
- What dangers are there in not waiting for direction from God?

Forget About It

Karen

"For I will be merciful toward their iniquities, and I will remember their sins no more."

—HEBREWS 8:12 ESV

In the midst of a heated conflict, do you ever get historical? Not hysterical, as in acting out of control, but historical—as in bringing up the past and rehashing previous wrongdoings and offenses.

"You'll never change!" "You're acting just like you did when . . ." "There you go again. You always . . ."

I do this to others. But mostly I do this to myself.

At times I have trouble remembering the name of the person I just met. However, I'm keenly adept at remembering my mistakes from the past. I can recount my sins as easily as I can recite the alphabet. When it comes to God, however, we don't have to fear He will bring up our past sins and use them against us, throwing them in our face and refusing to forgive. God said, "I will be merciful toward their iniquities, and I will remember their sins no more" (Hebrews 8:12 ESV).

This verse reminds me of a story of a man who claimed to have frequent dreams in which God visited him and they talked. He shared this with his pastor, who doubted whether this was actually true. So the pastor issued the man a challenge to help him prove whether or not his claims were valid.

"The next time God visits you," he instructed the man, "ask Him to tell you the worst sin I've ever committed." Since this pastor had a wild background, he knew God had a lot of sins to choose from.

Later when the pastor saw the man, he asked him, "Well, did God visit with you again?" The man replied, "Yes, He sure did."

"Okay, then tell me: what did He say was the worst sin I ever committed?"

The man responded, "When I asked, God looked straight at me and simply stated, 'Hmmm . . . I don't remember.'"

God's Word tells us, "He has removed our sins as far from us as the east is from the west" (Psalm 103:12 NLT). He not only removes sins; He forgets them! His ability to forget is His way of giving us a new start. He hits the refresh button on our lives and enables us to start over, no matter what grievous wrongs we've committed or how frequently we've committed them.

We must simply confess our sins to Him. He is faithful to forgive our wrongdoings, giving us a fresh beginning.

Perhaps it's time we "forget about it" just like God does. If He chooses not to remember our sins, why do we keep shaming and blaming ourselves for them?

Dear Lord, help me grasp the truth that You don't remember my sins. Thank You for not only forgiving my sins, but for forgetting them as well. May I live as a new creation, holy and blameless, as I seek to serve You. In Jesus' name, Amen.

- Ask God to bring to your mind things for which you have not forgiven yourself. Write these down in pencil. Then erase what you wrote, mirroring God's ability to forgive *and* forget.

Focus on What Matters Most

Ruth

Teach us to number our days, that we may gain a heart of wisdom.

—Psalm 90:12

I was ready to put our calendar in the shredder! Well, maybe not literally. But I was tired of so many obligations. All of the dates felt suffocating. There were too many things to do, places to go, ball games to attend, and events to remember. All of these appointments, opportunities, and commitments were invading family time.

Ever felt that way? My husband and I were talking about this just recently. It was summer, and we couldn't believe how fast it was flying by. It felt like every other night we had a sports activity. Or our kids were asking to have a friend spend the night. Or friends were asking our kids to spend the night. We just wanted to push pause. Slow down. Catch our breath.

Our family needed some boundaries to make our days count. They were going too fast, like sand slipping through our fingers. And so my husband and I decided to sit down with a blank piece of paper and begin asking some hard questions about how we spend our time—questions that we hoped would bring clarity, purpose, and boundaries. We needed these questions to help us live on purpose, more proactively and less reactively.

What is most important for our family right now?

What is God's heart for our kids when they leave our home?

How often will we try to eat dinner together?

How many sports or activities during a calendar year will we allow our kids to be involved in?

How often will we allow sleepovers?

These are just a few of the questions we began asking to help us slow down and bring clarity to what God wants for our family. Because everyone's circumstances are different, each family has to seek God's wisdom for their unique situations.

So we wrote down a few ideas that would serve as a bit of an anchor. These parameters aren't absolutes, but they are values. They are convictions that we need to clarify as a family. We needed to protect what is most important to us in this busy season of life.

What about you? Is God calling you to clarify your values and protect your time?

Father, teach me to number my days. Give me clarity about what You want for my family. Help us live on purpose so that we will honor You in all we do. In Jesus' name, Amen.

- What activity is invading your schedule right now?
- Would you say your family lives proactively or reactively? Why?
- What values might help you establish boundaries to protect family time?

With My Bible Pressed to My Heart

Karen

Search me [thoroughly], O God, and know my heart; Test me and know my anxious thoughts; And see if there is any wicked or hurtful way in me, And lead me in the everlasting way.

—Psalm 139:23–24 AMP

It was an ordinary day. My friend Laurel decided, as she often does, to spend some afternoon time reading her Bible and connecting with God in the midst of her busy day as a wife and mother. As she leaned forward to reach for something with one hand, she held her open Bible close to her heart with the other. It was then that it happened. Through the leather-bound book pressed upon her heart, she felt a small lump on her chest.

She saw a doctor and took numerous tests; Laurel's worst fear became reality. She had breast cancer.

The days, weeks, and years that followed brought hospital visits and radiation, probing and prodding, uncertainty and discomfort. Now, years removed from those emotionally trying days, my sweet friend's body is free from any traces of that often-deadly disease. She's a healthy high school foreign language teacher who goes about her days with a deep love for Jesus and profound gratitude in her heart. Most of all, she is thankful that God had arranged circumstances in such a way that her cancer was caught early because she had held her Bible close to her heart.

I recently pondered Laurel's experience. Embedded in a touchy relationship issue with a friend, I was angry. In this situation I felt used, violated, and unappreciated. I was ready to enter my alone time with God with a whine on my lips and an intense need to vent my mounting frustrations. It was then that He brought Psalm 139:23–24 to my mind.

I looked these verses up in the Amplified Version (which sheds light on the original Hebrew or Greek meaning of the words). It was then that my eyes fell upon this phrase: "See if there is any wicked or hurtful way in me, and lead me in the everlasting way" (AMP).

Instead of complaining about the actions of my friend, I decided to hold God's Word close to my heart, to see if there was any wicked or hurtful way in me, not in her. When I did, He was quick to point out ways I was wrong: deeply rooted attitudes I displayed that rear their ugly heads and manifest themselves in awful, unattractive behaviors—behaviors no Jesus-following woman should exhibit. I saw I was as much to blame in the situation, maybe even more to blame than my friend was.

With Scripture as His scalpel, God performed open-heart surgery on me that day. Now when I go to the Great Physician for regular checkups, He is faithful to point out the errors of my ways, to nudge me to allow His thoughts to radiate my soul, burn out the nasty disease that tries to take root and grow like a cancer, killing friendships and love.

I wonder just how many relational diseases could be cured if we were all more intentional, early on in the situation, to press our Bibles close to our hearts, feeling for any festering lumps of sin?

Dear Lord, please help me to love unconditionally and to tend to my own sin. In Jesus' name, Amen.

→ Have you ever been in a situation where God's Word—held up to your heart—caused you to see something in a relationship that needed attention? What happened?

- Is there a situation or relationship in your life that needs to be held up to the light of Scripture today?

Not Perfect, But Good

Ruth

The LORD God took the man and put him in the Garden of Eden to work it and take care of it.

—GENESIS 2:15

If it's any encouragement to you, there was only one perfect home—and that one didn't last long! It was far better than anything you've seen in the magazines. Rivers, trees, plenty of room for the kids to run around—there's a reason it was called *Eden,* which means "delight."

However, the sacred space created by God and for God would be transformed from a place of beauty into a battlefield. It was the home where the enemy first aimed to disrupt.

From the time of their first sin, Adam and Eve would have to work to have a home—similar, but very different than the one they once had. It wouldn't be perfect, but it could still be good.

Do you ever struggle with wanting to have the perfect home? Like the one you see in the designer magazines, on Pinterest, or on HGTV? I know I do!

Several years ago my husband and I returned from a date night to find that our babysitter had put dish soap in the dishwasher, and the kitchen had flooded with bubbles and water. Oops! This alone would not have been terribly disappointing had it not been for the brand-new laminate flooring we had just installed in the kitchen. So buckling floors were just another imperfection to add to the list of things that seemed to be wrong with our home.

Moving into a house that was more than a hundred years old had proved to be challenging. It needed a lot of work, but although we were young and expecting our first child, my husband and I went for it. Ten years later we had vowed we would never again buy a fixer-upper!

To many, our home seemed small, but to us, it was perfect. Not perfect in the sense that it was lacking flaws, bumps, or bruises. There were plenty of those! But perfect in that it was our home. It was our space—the place where we did life.

We don't always need more square footage, new appliances, or better accessories to have a beautiful home. The life lived inside a home—the love, the laughter, the joy, the struggles, the prayers, the good, and the bad—makes it beautiful. Though our home is far from perfect, it's good. And it's exactly where God has placed us to live for Him and with Him.

Father, help me to be content with where You have me. Teach me to see that a home is far more than stuff. Give me the strength and wisdom to make it beautiful. Fill it with Your presence, for Your purposes. In Jesus' name, Amen.

- When and why have you struggled with wanting to have the perfect home?
- Why is it hard at times for you to be content with your home?
- How can you make your home beautiful with your presence instead of with new things?

Low-Drama Dings

Karen

It does not dishonor others, it is not self-seeking, it is not easily angered, it keeps no record of wrongs.

—1 Corinthians 13:5

You know that moment as a mom when you want to squeal your van tires and flee the scene of whatever your child just ruined?

You know what I'm talking about. Maybe your son wet his pants on the new reading sofa at the library. Maybe it was the time your daughter knocked a jar of jam off the shelf at the new baking boutique, or maybe your kid said something out loud that was never meant to be spoken to another living creature.

In any of these cases, you feel like loading everyone into the vehicle and burning rubber all the way back to your unbreakable-décor, well-worn-fabric-filled home where you won't have to pay for damages.

That was exactly this feeling I was experiencing in the grocery store parking lot. It was a windy day, and as one of my children opened the passenger-side door, a strong gust of wind blew it wide open and into the neighboring vehicle.

I nonchalantly sauntered over to the other driver's car. I looked down and found what I had hoped I wouldn't find: a huge silver ding on the beautiful navy blue paint.

I gave the owner my most heartfelt apology. Then I waited for some kind of verbal or nonverbal backlash. She smiled and said, "No, don't you worry at all!" She put her groceries in the back of her car while I climbed into mine. I waited to see her shock when she finally saw how bad the dent was, but she never even looked at her door—not even once! She hopped in and drove off, and there was such a lack of drama that I just sat there stunned.

I don't know if that woman knows Jesus, but I had a church service in the parking lot! When that woman declared, "Don't worry about it," she really meant it! The whole scenario reminded me of 1 Corinthians 13:5, which says that love "is not easily angered, it keeps no record of wrongs." If that woman is a Christian, she showed the love of Jesus that day.

Our best form of outreach will be performing low-drama actions in highly practical ways when another response might've been completely expected. May we have church services in parking lots, coffee shops, and drive-throughs across the nation, showing love at first sight *and* forgetting at first slight.

Dear heavenly Father, may I understand love from You in such a tangible way that I can freely share it with others every day. Let me keep no record of wrongs with the people I have just met or the family members I've known for a long time. Help me love like You. In Jesus' name, Amen.

- Has someone ever extended grace to you when one of your kids ruined or damaged an item? Or, on the flip side, has someone ever blown their stack when something similar happened?
- How does being on the receiving end of either grace or grumpiness make you feel?
- How can it help you to remember such feelings when someone else (or her kiddos) damages your property?

Abide Even When You Can't Get Alone

Ruth

"Remain in me, as I also remain in you. No branch can bear fruit by itself; it must remain in the vine. Neither can you bear fruit unless you remain in me."

—JOHN 15:4

A few weeks ago I arose earlier than everyone else in hopes of stealing some alone time to read my Bible. As I settled in on the couch with my hot cup of coffee and Bible, I heard the tap-tap-tap of little feet making their way down the stairs.

For a moment my heart sank. So much for my alone time! But then I was instantly grateful for that sound, for those were the sweet feet of my youngest daughter, the child whom God had formed and entrusted to my care.

As you already know, being a mom is a calling to selflessness. In a real sense as moms, we not only have kids, but our kids have us.

They have our attention.

They have our devotion.

They have our affection.

They have our energy.

They have our time.

For all the joy that motherhood brings, the give-and-take can leave many moms feeling weary, overstretched, and empty. We have to be careful that we are receiving as well as giving.

So how do you stay strong and able to give? How do you continue giving of yourself to those precious little ones who need you? Where does the power come from to keep growing a healthy and God-honoring marriage in this busy season of life?

The answer isn't getting away; the answer is abiding more deeply.

As moms, we are called to shepherd and shape our children, but there is no formula for keeping our personal quiet time with the Lord a priority. Leaning into God's calling on our lives and grabbing those moments alone with Him when we can is vital. Although I know the need for quiet time, now four children later, I can still struggle to find those moments alone with God. My children will grow, but I will never outgrow my need to abide in Christ.

As busy mamas who give and give and give, we must be sure to fill up so we have something to pour into those around us. The task of being a mom is too big and overwhelming to try to do in our own strength. If we don't fill up, we will quickly dry up.

Be encouraged that God has promised to give us mercy and grace when we need it most (Hebrews 4:16). Lean into your calling, but don't neglect to abide deeply with your Father.

Father, I need Your grace today. I need You to quiet my heart. Draw me to You. Help me to stay close, to remain in You. Bear fruit in me that will nourish and strengthen my family. May they know I have been with You before I am with them today. In Jesus' name, Amen.

- What changes in your schedule do you need to make to abide more closely with Christ?
- What rhythms or spiritual disciplines (reading, fasting, prayer, solitude, worship) might help you abide during this season of your life?

→ What can you and your spouse do to give each other space and time to abide in your relationship with Christ?

Motherabilia

Karen

Mary treasured up all these things and pondered them in her heart.

—Luke 2:19

Do you ever feel like your kids are perpetual keepsake generators? Between church and VBS crafts, art-class renderings, and toilet-paper-roll structures, there's always something they want you to display, take a picture of, or keep. And that's just the beginning. First lost tooth, first locks of hair from a haircut, first blanket, first bib . . . !

Everything a child uses or produces can become a keepsake to us moms. We love our kiddos and, therefore we love what they do. Since we love what they do, we want to keep it—forever. That forever storage area can be the attic, the basement, extra memory space on various devices, or online folders where we hoard scads of photos. Motherabilia can take many forms.

And such memory hoarding can be exhausting. Trying to handle all the pictures, scrapbooks, memory bins, time capsules, entertaining quotes, and whatever else is just tiring. I know some moms get a thrill out of preserving memories, but I guess I missed out on that gene.

During the packing process as we prepared for our last move, we had to get rid of some things. We flat out didn't have space for them. As I threw away some great memorabilia, I wondered if I was doing anything wrong. I don't want to be a mom who constantly throws away keepsakes. I also don't want to keep things around that are not necessities.

A friend mentioned Luke 2:19 to me: "Mary treasured up all these things and pondered them in her heart." My friend said, "Mary kept these things in her heart, not her attic." I chuckled, but then I thought about it. The heart is where we ponder the precious times with our kids. The heart is where we treasure and store the memories of life. When our days on earth are finished, we can't take our scrapbooks with us.

Matthew 6:21 reminds us, "Where your treasure is, there your heart will be also." Maybe we need to spend less time physically documenting our activities and more time prayerfully treasuring time with our kids. As we go to God—thanking Him for the precious times with our children—we properly put our heart in the right place, centered on God and grateful for the important people in our lives.

Dear heavenly Father, please grant me the wisdom to know how to celebrate the moments but let go of the motherabilia. Let me never hold on to anything tighter than I hold on to You. In Jesus' name, Amen.

- Have you been spending lots of time trying to physically tuck away memories of your kids? Explain.
- What thoughts come to mind when you read that Mary "treasured up all these things and pondered them in her heart"? What might that treasuring in your heart look like for you?

Measuring Up

Ruth

Godliness with contentment is great gain.

—1 Timothy 6:6

We're wired to make comparisons. Have you seen this with your own kids? They compare bicycles, new shoes, biceps, dresses, how fast they can run, how high they can jump, and how many friends they have.

Just a few weeks ago I bought my youngest son new shoes. Do you remember the age when you thought new shoes meant running faster? Well, he's at that age! Suddenly his new shoes were the means by which he could compete against his friends.

We don't have to teach comparison or, for that matter, competition. Comparison comes easily. At a young age, I was no different. I remember comparing my cheerleading talent, my popularity, my clothing, and even my grades. I was just as guilty as my kids are. The sad thing? Even today as a mom, I can still fall into comparing.

As we grow up, or at least grow older, the points of comparison are different, but the comparisons continue. And we almost always compare ourselves to people we are most similar to.

Musicians listen to other musicians. Athletes compare themselves not against electricians or lawyers, but against other athletes. Follow that progression and you realize that, yes, parents are no exception.

We live in an increasingly competitive culture, so comparisons come easily and seem to be encouraged. Our sin tempts us to take our eyes off of Jesus and look at those around us. We compare our mothering, our kids, our homes, the books we read, our spiritual journeys, and a host of checklists we create.

Peel back the mask, and what you will often find is that the true face of comparison is either a heart of fear or a heart of pride. Maybe even both. Sometimes we peek into the lives of others to see how we're measuring up.

Are you struggling in this area? Is envy or discontentment knocking on your door? Do you often struggle to have joy when someone else succeeds? If so, you, too, may be struggling with comparing when you shouldn't be.

Life is not a race, and the world is not our judge. God is our Father, who in Christ has given us far beyond what we deserve. So we need to be careful of comparing—it might be saying more about our hearts than we realize.

Don't let the race marked out for someone else diminish the uniqueness of who you are and where God has called you. In all things, look to Jesus, and find rest in knowing that you are His.

Father, forgive me for often comparing myself to others. Teach me contentment. Help me look to You to find my peace and security. Your approval matters more than anyone else's. In Jesus' name, Amen.

- When was the last time you found yourself making comparisons with someone else or struggling with envy? What prompted that?
- Why do you think you struggle with being content?
- What causes you to compare yourself to others? Fear, pride, insecurity, or envy?

Drowning Out Distractions

Karen

I will listen to what God the Lord says; he promises peace to his people, his faithful servants—but let them not turn to folly.

—Psalm 85:8

I'm the lightest of sleepers, and being awakened at night by noises can mean utter exhaustion. That's why I love my white-noise machine, a little electronic contraption that sits beside my bed. It's my nightly sanity-saver.

Before I obtained this clever contraption, I lost sleep due to a snoring spouse or midnight-snacking teenager. As a result, I was cranky and cantankerous, frazzled and fruitless. As a sleep-deprived soul, I became unproductive, easily distracted, and downright ineffective.

Thankfully, now my nocturnal helper ushers me quickly to la-la land (and allows me to stay there) with one of its many options: waves crashing, birds chirping, or a thunderstorm gently rolling in. The constant stream of soothing sound drowns out any noise.

I've found a similar principle to be true in our spiritual lives. If we want to listen to God through prayer, study the Bible, and simply sit still before Him, we must drown out all distractions.

When our screaming schedules, messy houses, stacks of bills, or idle pastimes such as television or the Internet aren't intentionally blocked out, we will never find time in the day to rest and receive direction from God each day.

Jesus Himself was a master at drowning out distractions. A quick read through the New Testament will find Him often withdrawing to a lonely corner, getting up early to pray, or locating a place of calm focus amidst a clanging throng of people. Jesus purposed to find peace among the pandemonium.

Likewise in the Old Testament, the psalmists often list peace, calm, and quiet as gifts given to those who earnestly seek the Lord and desire to walk in His ways.

Embedded in Psalm 85:8 is such a promise to us as well: peace to God's people. But the precursor to experiencing that peace is listening to what the Lord has to say. And for listening to occur, we have to be able to hear from God, focused and free from all that clamors for our attention.

So, just as I plug in my slumber device each night, we must also unplug for a time each day. Shut off the phone, TV, laptop, and iPad. Ignore the dishes, paperwork, and pressing schedules so we can drift off to a peaceful place where sweet Jesus is waiting. He invites us to be still and listen long enough to actually hear Him speak to us.

Noise from so many daily distractions can keep us from hearing God's voice. Let's purpose together to drown out our distractions and tune in to the life-giving Word. He is the only Source of true and lasting peace.

Dear Lord, give me courage to unplug, determination to focus, and patience to listen. I want to bask in Your peace and walk in Your ways. In Jesus' name, Amen.

- What distractions in your day keep you from finding peace?
- What can you do differently today to pull away from the distractions and move toward God and His Word?

The Gift of Encouragement

Ruth

God, who encourages those who are discouraged,
encouraged us by the arrival of Titus.

—2 Corinthians 7:6 NLT

Six weeks after I gave birth to our youngest son, Noah, something didn't feel right in my stomach. The uncomfortable sensation soon turned into pain. And then agony! Before I knew it, I was back in the hospital. This time it was not to give birth but to have my appendix taken out.

Lying in a hospital bed just six weeks after having my third child, I was overwhelmed, discouraged, exhausted, and physically depleted. We've all been there. Discouragement hits us for different reasons and at different times.

We get sick.

We feel like nobody sees or appreciates what we do.

We feel like we're failing.

Busyness and stress sap us of energy and joy.

All of us know too well the feeling of discouragement. Everybody faces it. And especially during motherhood, it's easy to feel the weight of the world. What lifted me up during that season of childbirth and surgery was the encouragement of others.

It came in the form of flowers. A friend stopping by. A simple gift. A beautiful, thoughtful note from my women's Bible study group. The generosity of some students who cleaned our house. The remedy for my *dis*couragement was the *en*couragement of others. It gave me just what I needed to get up and keep going.

Just as we need encouragement, so do the other moms in our life. They, too, are likely struggling. The apostle Paul said we serve the God who "encourages those who are discouraged." And then he immediately told us that he was encouraged by the visit of his dear friend and partner in ministry, Titus.

One of the primary ways God encourages the discouraged is through His people. We are instruments He often uses to lift others up.

So who around you is struggling? Which moms in your neighborhood, school, church, or community need your encouragement? Maybe you can send a note, deliver a home-cooked meal, offer to watch her kids, or make a simple phone call. God wants to use you to encourage another mom today.

Father, thank You for refreshing my soul. Thank You for being the God of encouragement. I know that in Christ, and through Christ, You are my real joy. Help me have eyes to see those for whom I can be an instrument of love and support. In Jesus' name, Amen.

- When are you usually most susceptible to discouragement?
- What are some ways you can overcome discouragement?
- Whom can you encourage today?

God Is Not Worried

Karen

You can go to bed without fear; you will lie down and sleep soundly. You need not be afraid of sudden disaster or the destruction that comes upon the wicked, for the LORD is your security.

—PROVERBS 3:24–26 NLT

As a little girl I loved being outdoors. I liked to splash in puddles and jump in piles of leaves. However, there was one aspect that I didn't particularly care for: the critters. Spiders were scary; dogs, terrifying. And I couldn't even bear the thought of snakes. My intense fear of these creatures often kept me from fully engaging in play.

Unfortunately, even when I didn't encounter creepy-crawlies outdoors, they occasionally wound up in my dreams at night. I would have the recurring nightmare of snakes slithering toward me while I froze, unable to run away. I thought my fears would never go away until the one summer when I had no other choice.

The summer I turned twenty, I took a job at a nature center teaching preschoolers. I had to capture insects to examine and release, scoop tadpoles to study pond life, and even hold the snakes that were kept in glass tanks in the main building.

Although everything in me wanted to run away, there were little eyes on me. So I whispered a prayer for strength, pushed past my fears, and made those kids think I was a critter-lovin' instructor whose calm demeanor (and lack of screaming!) showed them there was nothing to fear. If their teacher wasn't freaking out, why should they?

Even though I worked through my fear that summer, as an adult now, I'm still tempted to freak out in fear. My imagination concocts all sorts of scenarios peppered with dread and doom. Sometimes I can't shake the fear as I try to fall asleep.

But I have come to trust this perspective-shifting truth: God is not worried. He's not in heaven wringing His hands, wondering how everything will eventually turn out. He is in control.

God longs to use the circumstances of our lives to mold our mind, craft our character, and chase away the fears that threaten to slither in, paralyzing us and rendering us ineffective. Ever the patient and wise Teacher, if He isn't freaking out, why should we?

Proverbs 3:24–26 is a sweet promise to us; however, these verses don't promise that we won't ever encounter disasters in life. But they do reassure us that we have no need to fear them. Why? Because the Lord is our security. He will be there to comfort and guide as He teaches us the lessons we need to learn.

With God as our security, we can have peace in the present. With God as our security, we can face the future without fear. And we can share this confidence we gain to inspire others, helping to keep them from unnecessary fret and worry.

Dear Lord, help me place my fears in Your hands, knowing You alone are my security, both now and in the future. In Jesus' name, Amen.

→ Is there a situation you're anxious about? Take it to God in prayer now. As part of your prayer, read Proverbs 3:24–26 out loud.

Walking in God's Word

Ruth

Blessed is the one who does not walk in step with the wicked or stand in the way that sinners take or sit in the company of mockers, but whose delight is in the law of the Lord, *and who meditates on his law day and night.*

—Psalm 1:1–2

"One, two, three, *four!* . . . Four steps!" my husband shouted.

By the sound of the cheering and screaming, you would have thought we were cheering our daughter on in her first marathon. But instead we were counting and celebrating her first steps.

Like most parents with little ones, we had cleared some of the furniture out of our family room. Too many large wooden objects were perfect opportunities for a trip to the ER. "Let's try it again," we yelled. "One, two, three, four . . ."

Those first steps were big steps. As most parents would be, we were excited that our child was finally walking. Those first small, clumsy steps were giant steps to us. Who knew something as simple as walking could be so exciting to a parent?!

It's no coincidence that the Bible frequently uses the language of walking. Learning to walk isn't something we do only as children. Sometimes simply taking the right steps can also be difficult for us as adult followers of Christ. We shouldn't be so surprised that we have a Father who delights in our steps, cheers us on, and advises us on the journey. Walking matters to God. Obedience to His Word happens a step at a time. "One, two, three, four!"

This is one of the reasons our family loves Psalm 1 so much. In fact, it's one of the first passages of Scripture we teach our children when they are old enough to begin memorizing Bible verses.

Psalm 1:1–2 is a particular passage that we have not only memorized but embraced as our family maxim. We come back to it often to remind ourselves to walk in wisdom and to remember the promises God gives us if we do so. We don't want our children to forget that. We want them to remember that when we walk in wisdom, we are like those beautiful trees that have an endless supply of water and are overflowing with fruit. We do our best to make that Scripture come alive for them.

As moms, we need to remember to keep cheering our children on as they learn God's Word. Don't give up. Don't quit moving forward. Let's keep putting one step in front of the other and teach our children to do the same.

"One, two, three, four!"

Father, give me strength to keep walking in Your Word. Teach me to cheer on my children as they follow after You. Give them a passion for Your truth. Thank You for holding us firmly in Your hand. In Jesus' name, Amen.

- What best describes your spiritual life right now: crawling, sitting, walking, or running? Explain.
- In what area of your life do you need the reminder and encouragement to keep putting one foot in front of the other?
- What can you do to cheer your children on as they learn to walk with the Lord?

Selfie-Centered

Karen

God is not unjust; he will not forget your work and the love you have shown him as you have helped his people and continue to help them.

—Hebrews 6:10

My friends and I giggled as we gathered around a new toy one of us had just purchased online—a selfie stick. This periscoping contraption allows several people to get into the frame of a cell phone camera to snap a picture of, well, ourselves! No more stretching out an arm and squeezing in tight. The selfie stick does the work for you!

Selfies are a simple way to capture a moment. We don't need a photographer, biographer, or reporter present. We can press a button, touch a few spots on the screen, and, in less than a minute, share a picture with the masses on the social media outlet of our choosing.

It's pretty cool. It's pretty commonplace. I just wonder why Jesus didn't do it. Obviously, I don't mean actual selfies since phones, cameras, and social media weren't invented yet. One thing that's been around for ages, however, is the human desire to keep an account.

I'm not sure why we're compelled to record our life, but our Savior didn't share this desire. I think it's because Jesus knew *His Father saw.* Jesus knew *His Father would share what is necessary*. Jesus knew *His Father wouldn't forget*. The following verses illustrate these truths.

"From heaven the Lord looks down and sees all mankind; from his dwelling place he watches all who live on earth—he who forms the hearts of all, who considers everything they do" (Psalm 33:13–15). *God sees.*

"Jesus did many other things as well. If every one of them were written down, I suppose that even the whole world would not have room for the books that would be written" (John 21:25). *God knows what's worthy of sharing.*

"God is not unjust; he will not forget your work and the love you have shown him as you have helped his people and continue to help them" (Hebrews 6:10). *God doesn't forget that which should be remembered.*

God knows what can fall away forever and what is worth chronicling. Whether we fill our feed with selfies or have no feed at all, let's evaluate *why* we do *what* we do. The Savior of the world lived the life most worthy of viral posts. He deserved the most friend requests, retweets, and trending topics, yet He never promoted Himself. Jesus lived life such that others had to share His story. We could be that way too.

Dear heavenly Father, help me trust You with the details of my life. You see everything. Let me share You more than I share me. In Jesus' name, Amen.

- How frequently do you capture and share with the social media world the events of your day?
- What percentage of time would you say you post so others know what hard work you are doing as a mom, wife, employee, or volunteer?
- Are there times you should allow God to be your only audience? If so, at what times and why?

A Little Temple

Ruth

Continue in what you have learned and have become convinced of, because you know those from whom you learned it, and how from infancy you have known the Holy Scriptures, which are able to make you wise for salvation through faith in Christ Jesus.

—2 Timothy 3:14–15

After the temple in Jerusalem was destroyed in 70 A.D., many of the Jewish leaders began to refer to the home as a *miqdash me'at* (a small or little temple). I've always loved this picture because it reminds parents not only how safe our home should be, but also how sacred it should be.

The home is the place where Jesus stands at the center. It's a refuge or shelter from all that's going on outside. But it's also a place of worship where God's truth is passed on from one generation to the next. We make it home by filling it with our presence. It is a place marked off for meaningful relationships, intentional love, Christlike guidance, and heartfelt joy. As moms, we have the privilege of building that kind of home for our family.

What kind of home are you building? Is it your dream home? Is it your castle? Or is it a "little temple," a place carved out from the rest of the restless world?

I can't help but wonder what our kids will remember about home. I pray they will remember our home as somewhere special and sacred—a place where Mom and Dad weren't always perfect but Jesus was present and pursued. More than just information, we want our children to experience transformation because of Jesus, our great Lord and Savior!

It's never too early to begin cultivating a love for Jesus in the life of your child. God wants to work through you as a mom to show His love and extend His peace in your home.

Father, let my home be a place where we are aware of Your presence. Let it be a sanctuary that Your joy, love, peace, and truth fill. Help me create sacred space for my family. Let it be a refuge from everything else we face. In Jesus' name, Amen.

- How would you describe the climate of your home?
- Why are your attitude and behavior so critical for creating sacred space in your home?
- What are several ways you can make your home feel more like a "little temple"?

____

____

____

____

____

You're Always Doing That

Karen

In Joppa there was a disciple named Tabitha, which is translated Dorcas. She was always doing good works and acts of charity.

—ACTS 9:36 HCSB

"Mom, stop! You're always doing that!" my then twelve-year-old daughter pleaded with me one Tuesday morning. She was about to head out the door to her homeschool co-op, but I saw a slight problem. I thought she had on too much sparkle lip gloss, and her peachy-pink blush was a little heavy for my liking. And so I took it upon myself to rub her blush in a little and make her blot her lips on a tissue to tone down her preteen makeup.

There are many other motherly actions that I'm sure—if you polled my dear offspring—you'd discover that I'm "always doing." Reminding them to wear their seatbelts. Telling them never to talk to strangers online. Delivering my famous mama lecture each time I drop them off at a friend's house or at school: "Be sure your sins will find you out." (That truth from Numbers 32:23 was my mama's own sermon to me each day when I was a kid.) Or I'm always looking for delicious recipes on Pinterest. Or asking my kids' new friends to tell me their "whole life story." (Hey, I'm just trying to be friendly!)

In the book of Acts, we meet a woman from the town of Joppa. Her name was Tabitha, which is translated *Dorcas* in Greek. She isn't one of the well-known Bible women such as Eve, Sarah, or Mary, the mother of Jesus. She only pops up on the pages of Scripture in this book, her name simply stitched into a few short verses. Although she isn't a well-known Bible gal, she *was* well known for something during the time her sandals were shuffling about the earth. She was identified for "always doing good works and acts of charity" (HCSB).

If someone were following us around with the intent to chronicle our actions for future generations, could the same be said of us?

Perhaps we can learn a little lesson from our ancient sister Dorcas. Might we as moms start to strategically, yet simply, work into our days doing good and performing acts of charity? What would this look like?

It might mean that when you bake cookies for your own family, you habitually bake an extra batch to take over to the next-door neighbors or to send to your child's teacher, coach, or bus driver. Or, when trekking off to get your groceries, you always check with the elderly couple from church to see if they need anything from the store. Maybe it's taking your brood on a Saturday morning once a month to serve breakfast at a soup kitchen or to help with yard work for a single mom so she can spend time with her kids instead.

How about it? Wouldn't you like it to be said of you, "She's always doing such thoughtful things!"? May we, like Dorcas, reach out to others with acts of kindness and charity, modeling thoughtfulness for our children.

Father, may I always be on the lookout for those who need a helping hand. Please create opportunities for me to love like You. In Jesus' name, Amen.

- When was the last time you performed an act of kindness for someone or did charitable work?
- What can you plan for your family this month that will give them the opportunity to help out those who are in need?

Praying When You Feel Powerless

Ruth

Rejoice always, pray continually, give thanks in all circumstances; for this is God's will for you in Christ Jesus.

—1 THESSALONIANS 5:16–18

Long before I became a Christian, I started praying. As a young child, I wasn't really sure who I was praying to or even why, but I knew how small I was. And I was scared. Overwhelmed. Worried about the future. And so I did what most people do when they feel like they're in over their heads: I cried out for help! I started praying because I knew I was powerless.

Little did I know at the time that God, in His timing, would answer some of those childlike prayers. More than giving me all the answers, He would give me Himself. As a Christian, I would begin to learn and know that God is far from an impersonal force running the world.

He is a Father who is strong when He needs to be. His heart is tender; He is full of compassion and grace. In Christ, He has promised never to leave me or forsake me. His wisdom, strength, and resources are far beyond my own.

And though I know Him better today, one thing has not changed: I'm still powerless. This is why I keep praying. All of the demands, concerns, and real-life issues of marriage and parenting are enough to keep me on my knees!

I think this is why God's Word tells us to pray—and pray often. We are to pray without ceasing; we are to pray "continually." We are to live with an awareness of not only our own weakness, but God's strength and closeness.

Prayer is not a task I check off but a constant communication I'm blessed to have. While longer periods of prayer are great, I stay close to God by talking frequently with Him.

What are you scared of right now? What's overwhelming you? Do you feel powerless? If so, you are exactly where God wants you. He has made you to depend on Him, to draw from the depths of His provision and power. Whatever you are going through, and wherever He has led you, you are not alone. Your Helper is near. Cry out to Him. He loves us by listening to us and is faithful to respond according to our needs.

Father, teach me to trust You. Keep me from worry and from trying to do life on my own. I need You. You are wiser, stronger, and more able than I am to provide for all of my needs. Draw near to me today, as I draw near to You. In Jesus' name, Amen.

- How would you describe your prayer life in this season, and why?
- What are you struggling to trust God with?
- Why do you think it's so hard to pray continually?

The $285 Cinnamon Roll

Karen

Blessed are those who act justly, who always do what is right.

—Psalm 106:3

It was a simple cinnamon roll: a jumbo pastry from our local all-night diner laden with gooey cream cheese frosting.

The cost? Just $285.

My sixteen-year-old son was spending the night at a friend's house. At a little past dark, they got a hankering for this sweet treat and decided to make the two-mile trek to satisfy their culinary desire.

Our state has rules for sixteen-year-old drivers. They may not have more than one other person in the car unless that person is a relative. Also, they may not drive past 10:00 p.m. unless they're returning from school, church, or work.

The boys decided the nineteen-year-old should drive; however, his car was out of gas. So my son allowed him to drive our car instead. Upon leaving the restaurant, his friend discovered that he didn't have his driver's license with him. They decided it was better for my son to shuttle the gang home rather than for his friend to drive without his license.

The flashing lights of a police vehicle interrupted their trip home. My son got pulled over. Questioned. Busted. Not only was he driving past curfew, but he also had three unrelated passengers in the vehicle with him. He was fined heavily and ordered to take and pay for an online driving refresher course. Additionally, he had to appear before a judge at the Secretary of State's office.

Although the authorities told us the hearing is usually just a stern lecture (which my husband and I were glad he would get!), when my son's turn came, the judge listened to his story. And then? She took his driver's license away for two months and ordered him to pay a three-digit fine to get it back.

The diner's menu that fateful night listed the cinnamon roll for the meager price of $3 and some change. In the end, it actually cost our son a total of $285 dollars of his own hard-earned money because he didn't do the right thing by obeying the laws of our state.

Although we know we should "always do what is right" as Psalm 106:3 urges, sometimes we think we can bend the rules ever so slightly. We might even have good reasons, as my son felt he did that night. But rules are rules. Laws are laws. Breaking them comes with consequences—and sometimes with stiff penalties and hefty fines.

Likewise, we might bend God's rules. Flirt with sin. Rationalize wrongdoing. Things such as: *It's not really gossip if I'm simply sharing a prayer request. . . . I don't think of it as lying, just creatively leaving out a few minor details. . . . Come on! I'm just reconnecting with a former guy "friend" I found on Facebook for a cup of coffee. What harm could there be in that?*

Sin snowballs. And it often cruelly crushes those foolish enough to stand in its path.

When we're tempted to twist God's commands oh so slightly, let's remember my cinnamon-roll-craving son. What we think has an affordable price tag might end up costing us a whole lot more.

Father, please help me to pause before I decide to bend Your commands even a tiny bit. Give me the strength to make right and righteous choices. In Jesus' name, Amen.

- Was there a time that you bent the rules either legally or spiritually? What happened?
- What might you do differently today if you were placed in that same situation?

Building Wisely with Our Words

Ruth

A wise woman builds her home, but a foolish woman tears it down with her own hands.

—Proverbs 14:1 NLT

My dad is a builder. When I was growing up, he was always building or rebuilding something—a roof, a new room, a deck, or flooring. He was (and still is) very good at it. He has a skill for taking raw materials and transforming them into something useful and beautiful.

As wise women we are to build while the foolish tear down. We don't build with brick and mortar; we build with our words. Our words build others up and build meaningful, intimate relationships.

Our homes become a safe place—like a little sanctuary carved out from the noise, stress, chaos, and busyness of life. We build our homes into places where we invite friends in to be known and to know us. And it's with our words that our homes and relationships become a refuge.

The Bible teaches us that our words can be a tool for either life or death: with our words we'll either build our relationships or break them.

Do you have those friends who make you feel like someone has breathed fresh life into you when you are with them? Being with them is to be refreshed. Your presence together brings renewal. A friend who takes the time to offer life-giving words is a real treasure.

When we take the time to invest in deep, meaningful conversation, we build intimacy, trust, and comfort in our relationships. When we encourage one another with our words, we become great sources of joy and strength.

God has not called us to demolition work; He's called us to building! Let our words be like tools in the hands of a skilled carpenter. With God's help, let's build something beautiful, intimate, and renewing in our relationships using our words. Let our lives be a place where we invite true friendship to happen.

Father, may I remember the words You have spoken over me in Christ: I am loved, accepted, and treasured. May Your words surround me like a shield. Help me build my home and my relationships with words that bring life. In Jesus' name, Amen.

- How can you do a better job building up others using your words?
- How can you be more intentional to build friendships that are meaningful and intimate?

Coming Clean

Karen

Create in me a clean heart, O God, and renew a right spirit within me.

—Psalm 51:10 ESV

Oh, Jenny," I remarked to my friend, "you totally crack me up! All right then, we'll see you next week."

With that, the expectant mom grabbed her purse and her Bible, gave me a quick hug, and dashed out the door. She'd just announced to our Bible study group that her mother-in-law was coming to town for a few days and would be arriving later that night. Grandma was making the trip in order to assist her daughter-in-law with deep-cleaning her house. The nearly belly-busting mom was succumbing to what is fondly referred to as "nesting": that instinctive cleaning compulsion expectant moms have just prior to delivery or right before that wonderful trip to bring home their adopted child.

What gave me a chuckle that fall afternoon was what Jenny was actually headed home to do before her hubby's mom came to town. Was it to prepare a hot supper or to make room in a child's bedroom for Grandma's suitcase and such?

Nope. Jenny was speeding home so she could do one thing.

Clean her house.

Yep, clean her house. Just before her house-cleaning help arrived. Jenny said she didn't want to be embarrassed by any killer dust bunnies or cobwebs that might be lurking where Grandma could spy them. So Jenny was going to surface-shine as much as she could before her mother-in-law pulled out the big guns—aka vacuums and mops—to tackle the deep cleaning.

Perhaps we've all done something similar. Maybe, for example, we flossed our teeth for the first time in months just before our biannual dentist appointment. Something in us desperately doesn't want others to know just how dirty we actually let things get in our lives.

And this isn't just a matter of house cleaning and hygiene. An innate urge asserts we must somehow clean up our act before we can come to Jesus.

We feel it when we meet Him for the first time. Our bulky baggage of sin burdens us. So we try to clean up our act so we can then come to Him. But as that contemplative, shepherd-turned-psalmist David declared in Psalm 51:10, we need not attempt to spit-shine our own hearts, but rather we must plead, "Create in me a clean heart, O God" (ESV).

Yes, we do the pleading. He does the cleaning. Only then will the dust bunnies of darkness that can suffocate our souls be completely swept away so a renewed spirit can truly shine. What a wonderful and spiritually effective way to be taken to the cleaners!

Dear Lord, may I come to You, tarnish and all, trusting in Your ability to make my heart clean. In Jesus' name, Amen.

- Time to come clean! Do you feel like you must clean up your act before God will accept you?
- Take time now to pour your heart out to God—just as you are—knowing that He loves you and longs for you to be more like His Son. Remember, you do the pleading; He does the cleaning.

Creating Community

Ruth

They devoted themselves to the apostles' teaching and to fellowship, to the breaking of bread and to prayer.

—Acts 2:42

What do you think of when you hear the word *devoted*? I envision someone who is committed, determined, and loyal. The kind of person who is going to set his or her sights on something and see it through.

Maybe you picture a runner, student, business executive, or musician. Those who are devoted are not casual about their pursuit. I think this is why the word *devoted* in Acts 2:42 really strikes me.

Those early Christians were devoted to God's Word, devoted to sharing meals, devoted to prayer, but also devoted to one another. Community was essential for them. They possessed loyalty and diligence to be in community with others.

It's a beautiful picture, especially if you've read the entire book of Acts. You know that this young and growing church would share their lives, possessions, homes, successes, and even sufferings. They were deeply committed to one another.

As we have become a more connected culture, mainly through social media, we often are more disconnected from face-to-face community. Motherhood makes getting together with others even harder. Nursing babies, sick kids, busy schedules, and sheer exhaustion make community seem like a luxury.

But community is a necessity. We need others to help us keep pressing on. Doing life with others brings incredible joy. After all, relationships are what really matter most. However, here's what I've discovered: community doesn't happen accidentally.

The truth is, creating community takes work. It requires time and effort. And oftentimes it takes someone who is willing to step forward and initiate. If we sit back and wait for someone else to create community for us, it rarely happens.

So is God calling you to create meaningful community with others? How can you and your family take the first step and be the one to carve out community?

Life, and motherhood in particular, is too difficult to do alone. Stop waiting for others to invite you over! Take the first step. Get out the calendar. Set a date. Make some plans and start creating community. You will be so glad you did!

Father, You are the giver of good gifts. As Father, Son, and Spirit, You are the eternal relationship. Help me to model who You are by creating community with others. Give me courage to take the first steps in carving out space for others. In Jesus' name, Amen.

- Why is community so difficult to foster?
- How would community be a blessing to you right now?
- How can you begin to take the first step toward creating meaningful community?

Mistaken Identity

Karen

"Whoever belongs to God hears what God says."

—John 8:47

I poured a cup of coffee and logged on to my computer to peek at a friend's Facebook page. When I tried hopping over to see her latest pictures, her name didn't appear in the search bar. I was puzzled. Glancing at the top of the screen, I realized I wasn't logged in to my own account. My son had forgotten to sign off when he'd been on earlier, so I was actually logged in as him instead. I couldn't get where I wanted to go because I had a mistaken identity.

With a quick click of a mouse, I switched accounts and used Facebook as "me." Under the right identity, I was free to view friends' pages, leave comments, and get where I wanted to go.

Sometimes in life we encounter a similar issue. A mistaken identity keeps us from living out God's best for our lives. A voice from our past or our own negative self-talk may cause us to forget our identity in Christ. We log in to our day and encounter wrong thinking that's not in sync with who we are. Those wrong thoughts lead us to doubt God's love and miss out on the security He offers. We can question our value, which is rooted deep in His heart for us.

Instead of the truth about our identity, we hear: *You can't do that. You aren't good enough. You'll never change. Why can't you be more like your sister? If only you were more* __________ *instead of so* __________.

When self-doubt screams and discouragement sets in, we need to recognize what's happening, log out of the lies we believe, and log in to God's truth. It's only when we know our true identity in Christ that we can navigate our lives according to God's Word.

John 8:47 tells us, "Whoever belongs to God hears what God says." We need to listen to His Word, download it in our minds, and allow it to eradicate any untrue, destructive thought patterns. Replacing the negative chatter with reassuring Scriptures will gently but firmly remind us we are children of God.

Yes, if we belong to God, we will hear what He says. As we log in to His truths daily, no longer will we mistake our identity. We will know the confident reality of who we are in Christ.

Dear Lord, when I'm tempted to think of myself in a way that is neither healthy nor true, remind me both of who I am and to *whom* I belong. In Jesus' name, Amen.

- Have you ever struggled with feeling as though you've misplaced your spiritual identity? What contributed to that?
- What does John 8:47 say about your true identity in Christ?

Waiting for Your Prodigal

Ruth

"While he was still a long way off, his father saw him and was filled with compassion for him; he ran to his son, threw his arms around him and kissed him."

—LUKE 15:20

Being lost is scary. Who doesn't remember feeling alone, being disoriented, and finding yourself disconnected from what is secure and familiar?

I can still remember the first time I was lost. I let go of my dad's hand in a busy mall. I had stopped at a kiosk just long enough to look at some toys. When I looked up again, I suddenly found myself alone. Little did I know, my father was close by. He knew exactly where I was even when I lost sight of where he was.

As I read the Gospels, I'm especially reminded of how much God loves those who are lost, the ones who have let go of their Father's hand and wandered into unfamiliar territory, surrounded by real danger and unable to get back home.

In Luke 15, Jesus told three parables about being lost.

First it was a sheep.

Then a coin.

And finally a child.

I have always been struck by the effort involved in searching for those lost objects. The sheep didn't find its way back, nor did the coin wander out from under a table or couch. In each of these parables, Jesus illustrated the heart of a Father who not only loves the lost but is also actively looks for them.

Recently I was talking to a mom whose son is spiritually lost. He was nineteen when he let go of his Father's hand. She has not stopped praying for him, loving him, and still to this day, she's anxiously waiting for him to come home.

The good news is that God is not done looking for, pursuing, loving, and seeking those who are lost. Maybe you have a son or daughter who has walked away from faith. They have made choices that have taken them farther from God. Your heart is heavy with the weight of watching someone you dearly love run from the greatest Love of all.

If that is you, don't give up. Don't despair. God the Father is not far from your son or daughter. These children may have lost sight of Him, but He has not lost sight of them. He not only loves; He also looks for those who are lost, welcoming back prodigals just as He welcomed us.

Father, thank You for Your faithful love. Thank You for pursuing me. You are a Father who is patient but also persistent. You love the lost, and I trust You. Help me to trust Your power and Your timing. In Jesus' name, Amen.

- Why did Jesus tell three stories about something that was lost? What does that tell you about the heart of God?
- As you think about the story of the prodigal son, what does the father do that most surprises you?
- If you are the mom of a prodigal son or daughter, how can you trust God in this season?
- If you know a mom of a prodigal son or daughter, how can you encourage her today?

Juicy-Fruit Faith

Karen

Your wife will be like a fruitful vine within your house.

—Psalm 128:3

My friend Marcia has a grape arbor in her backyard. Each fall, the twisted, gnarly branches become laden with clusters of purple fruit. The grapes are quite sour and contain tiny seeds, but they make delicious homemade jelly and jam. One year my kids and I even picked a large basketful, pressed the grapes into juice, and used it for our family's communion time at home.

Oftentimes in the Bible we read about grapes and vines. The region of the world where many of the stories in the Bible take place is home to lots of vineyards. Since they are part of the landscape, they pop up many places in Scripture. Sometimes when we read over and over again about a common biblical item or practice, we don't always key in to the significance because it becomes so commonplace to us. When we read in Psalm 128 that a wife is "like a fruitful vine," we can skim over the phrase and miss an important lesson. So let's think a little bit about how grapes grow.

If you ask professional vinedressers what makes the plumpest and juiciest fruit around, they will tell you how important pruning is. Pruning is the process of cutting away dead or overgrown branches. Pruning the vines is imperative to maintaining the health and vigor of the plant because it affects the amount of sunlight reaching the leaves. The leaves need to drink in sunlight in order to grow the fruit to a juicy, ripe stage. Removing some of the clusters or diminishing the bulk of them also has a substantial effect on the size of the fruit. Twisted, overgrown grapevines produce tiny, poor-quality grapes. Properly pruned vines give way to gloriously plump, ripe, and useful fruit.

If we want to produce useful, wholesome fruit in our homes as wives and mothers, we must allow God to prune away that which is dead, lifeless, and energy-sapping. We must make room for the Son to shine so we can be properly nourished, grow deep roots, and produce juicy, faith-filled fruit in our lives. Taking time each day to ask the Lord to remove the dead weight in our hearts is so important. If we want to experience growth, we need to willingly allow God access to our hearts—even the dark and scorched places that we sometimes don't want anyone to see.

Let's not be afraid of the master Vinedresser. Yes, He comes with clippers, ready to prune away whatever is holding us back. Although the process may sting a little, it will help produce an abundant crop of fruit in our lives, fruit that will spill over and bless those we love most.

Father, forgive me for harboring in my heart that which keeps me from experiencing fruitful growth. I long for Your perfect pruning touch. Make me fruitful and useful for Your kingdom and for my family as well. In Jesus' name, Amen.

- Take a few moments today to sit quietly with God. Ask Him what dead weight you may be harboring in your heart: anger, resentment, jealousy, discontentment, or something else. Confess to Him anything that comes to mind in prayer. Then ask Him to prune away the sin and produce fruitful growth in your life.

Establishing Traditions

Ruth

There is a time for everything, and a season for every activity under the heavens.

—Ecclesiastes 3:1

Every Sunday night, our kids look forward to what we call Sunday Sundae. As the name might suggest, ice cream is involved. After dinner, we pick a favorite worship song from YouTube to sing together, do our family devotions, and then hurry to make ice cream sundaes. That's the not-so-spiritual part! Sunday Sundae has become one of our favorite family traditions.

As you read the Bible, you'll notice that God instructed His people to follow regular rhythms (minus the ice cream, of course!). In the Hebrew Scriptures, these rhythms were marked by yearly feasts, holidays, or appointed times. In the New Testament, we're told to "remember" and "proclaim" Jesus' death and resurrection as we gather regularly at the Lord's table.

These rhythms were meant to remind God's people of sacred traditions that communicated sacred truths. For example, on the Sabbath, they remembered that God is Creator and Sustainer. On the Day of Atonement, solemn in nature, they reflected on God as Judge. And on the more joyous celebration: the Feast of Booths, they were reminded of how God dwelled with them in the wilderness.

Each of these appointed times became a yearly tradition, when the people of God refocused on who God is and what He had done for them.

These celebrations served as a sacred calendar that was meant to keep the Israelites mindful of their Redeemer.

Traditions are powerful. As a family, you can create your own rhythms. Maybe you grew up in a home with memories of cutting down a tree at Christmas, picking out a turkey for Thanksgiving, or something as insignificant as getting matching pajamas each year.

One of my favorite family traditions was something small, or so it seemed. Every Sunday night my parents and I would drive across town to my grandparents' house. We ate dinner together, talked, worked on puzzles, played Skip-Bo, and enjoyed walks when the weather was nice. Long before I became a Christian, God was using this tradition to shape me and give me a vision for my own future family. Traditions, big or small, can leave a lasting imprint.

So what tradition can you create for your family? What rhythms, with sacred truth, can you establish for your children?

Simple traditions may not always seem like much to us, but they can be a lasting legacy for our children.

Father, help me create meaningful family moments. Teach me to wrap Your truths in sacred traditions. Use these moments to make memories. But more than memories, use our time together to help pass on faith to the next generation. In Jesus' name, Amen.

- What is the significance of God establishing rhythms for His people in the Bible?
- What family traditions were most meaningful to you when you were growing up?
- What is one tradition you can begin to establish in your family?

Where Am I in This?

Karen

Let each of you look not only to his own interests,
but also to the interests of others.

—Philippians 2:4 ESV

We stopped at a wayside rest area to get a little something to eat and stretch our legs a bit. It was a long trip from our home in the center of Michigan to my Aunt Patty and Uncle Lee's place in beautiful northern Wisconsin. This particular wayside had an interesting gift shop stocked with many items: fascinating gnarled pieces of driftwood, multicolored Native American artifacts, and more than a hundred varieties of seashells. Our three kids made their way down the aisles, studying the wonderful treasures before their eyes.

At the end of one aisle sat a spin rack displaying whimsical kitchen mugs personalized with first names. One of the boys spied it and alerted his siblings to this find. Soon all three kids were giving the rack a spin and looking for something. What was it?

You guessed it! Each of the kids was looking for his or her name on a mug—the string of letters that would spell out "me."

We've all done similar things. When we get our family reunion pictures, high school yearbook, or church pictorial directory, something within us drives us to pick up those items and determine, "Where am I in this?"

Sadly, we often live in a way that also says, "Me first!" Whether it's the plans for the coming weekend or the control of the television remote, what we really want to know—whether we verbalize it or not—is, "What's in this for me?"

Since we are followers of Christ, people around us should see us live out values that are the opposite of the world's values. The world says to look out for number one, climb over anyone you need to in order to reach the top, and pamper yourself on a regular basis. We who claim Christ should instead be the ones who go the extra mile, give the benefit of the doubt, and put others' desires ahead of our own. Others-centered, not self-centered.

Philippians 2:4 doesn't say that we are never to think about what we might need but that we should look *not only* to our own interests, but *also* to the interests of others. Taking care of yourself and your needs is fine. Just don't stop there. Take into account the other guy or gal too. Be friendly when you drive, gladly give up that close parking space; let someone else choose the restaurant; or allow that mom with screaming children to go ahead of you at the supermarket even though you have fewer items than she does. Let her go first, and pray for her as you wait.

Let's look for little ways to daily lay down our lives for others. It will make us less self-absorbed and more like Christ.

Dear Lord, may You gently nudge me as I walk through my day. Reveal tangible ways I can put others first. Shape my heart to look more like Yours. In Jesus' name, Amen.

→ What is one way you can live others-centered today rather than self-centered? Be specific. And then go do it!

Are You in the Desert?

Ruth

Remember how the Lord *your God led you all the way in the wilderness these forty years, to humble and test you in order to know what was in your heart, whether or not you would keep his commands.*

—Deuteronomy 8:2

The desert can be a dangerous place. In Bible times it was always a place of uncertainty, peril, trial, and death. Not the kind of place you want to go on vacation!

Several years ago my husband and I found ourselves in a desert place. My husband, a pastor, had just resigned from our church so we could plant a church with another pastor and his wife. Little did we know that the friend and pastor we were going to plant the church with would be diagnosed with cancer. My husband and I, along with our one-year-old child, had just moved to a different town to plant the church, and we were living with my in-laws while our home was for sale. When the church plant was suddenly called off, my husband took the first job available. It was a job we both knew wouldn't cover the bills long term. We were sinking, or so it felt.

During this trying time, I had my first miscarriage. We were experiencing disappointment and grief on all sides. Our situation seemed hopeless. I pleaded with God for direction and financial relief, and God provided. After six months of struggling that felt like forty years, we moved back to our old town, and my husband started a new full-time job in ministry.

During desert experiences we can too easily focus on our circumstances instead of God's character. We grow weary instead of waiting patiently. Yet God's Word reminds us, "Do not let your heart be troubled" (John 14:1). Believing that God is good and that He can take care of us through our desert experiences gives us hope and joy in the midst of our uncertainty.

When my feelings threaten to overshadow my trust in Him, I must turn my heart immediately to His promises. I remind myself that the Lord isn't slow to fulfill His promises (2 Peter 3:9). His ways are perfect (Psalm 18:30). God works all things for good (Romans 8:28). Just like He led the Israelites in the desert, He leads us.

Father, I know that You are good. I know that You are present with me, even in the hard places. So now, when I can't understand why I'm going through a desert place, help me cling to the promises You've given me in Scripture. Help me to remember that Your character doesn't change like my circumstances do. In Jesus' name, Amen.

- How is God testing you in your desert experience?
- What part of your character do you think God is trying to refine in this season?
- What promise from Scripture do you need to cling to during this time?

I Want All the Answers Now

Karen

They believed his promises and sang his praise. But they soon forgot what he had done and did not wait for his plan to unfold.

—Psalm 106:12–13

My son Mitchell was a curious child. When he first learned to talk, he often repeated the same three phrases to me: "Why?" "How?" and "When?"

His sparkly green eyes were always wide with wonder. When I cooked, he would drag a kitchen chair over to the stove and stand on it next to me. His inquiring mind needed to know the reason behind every ingredient I tossed in the pot. Why was I using brown eggs and not white ones? Why was I adding potatoes but not carrots? And speaking of carrots, why were they orange and not blue?

As Mitchell grew older, the questions continued. Soon after his feet hit the floor each morning, he wanted to know how the day would unfold. Were we going to the church picnic? What would we have to eat? Would the kids play football?

I couldn't possibly answer all his questions. What I could do was remind him that, no matter what happened, everything always turned out fine in the end. He just needed to trust that we had planned pleasant things for him to do.

I didn't want to squelch Mitchell's inquisitive spirit, but sometimes I wished he'd just relax and enjoy the ride instead of always wanting to know in advance all the details of each day.

When it comes to my own life, though, I'm a lot like my son. I want God to tell me what's going to happen next, explain how my life will unfold each day.

The ancient Israelites had a similar mind-set. Sometimes they trusted the Lord and stood on His promises. But often they wobbled and lost their footing. They had to know how. And when. And—most importantly—why?

Psalm 106:12–13 tells us, "Then they believed his promises and sang his praise. But they soon forgot what he had done and did not wait for his plan to unfold."

Scripture urges us to believe the promises of God. He knows what He's doing even if at times we're not sure that He does. And, yes, God is faithful even during the times when He seems to be silent.

When God doesn't give us explanations at each turn, it builds our faith. We must learn to trust even when we cannot understand. We can go to Him in prayer, asking Him to calm our anxious hearts. We can ask Him to increase our faith so we aren't consumed by the questions and so we can trust that He—the ever-wise Parent—has good in mind for us.

It is God's job to unfold our future. It is our job to do our best to make wise choices as we trust and glorify Him throughout the process. Let's stop asking Him to spiritually skywrite all the answers, and let's write His promises on our hearts instead.

And then? Let's live like we believe them.

Dear Lord, help me each day not to seek explanations of what You are doing in my life. Instead, may I seek a closer walk with You. In Jesus' name, Amen.

→ When have you most struggled with wanting God to continually answer "Why?" "How?" and "When?"

- What questions about your life do you most want God to answer? Why those in particular?

What's for Dinner?

Ruth

Be completely humble and gentle; be patient, bearing with one another in love.

—Ephesians 4:2

"What's for dinner?" my husband asked.

"Nothing. Just . . . nothing!" I sputtered out with a bit of impatience and frustration.

My husband broke into a fit of laughter. I didn't know whether to laugh or cry. So I asked him, "When would I have had time to think about dinner today?"

You see, we were leaving on our family vacation the next morning. I had been gone most of the day. Who needs dinner?! We had bags to pack, loose ends to tie up, and a house to put in order so we wouldn't return to a mess.

As I think about that silly exchange, I can't help but smile and be thankful for my marriage. My husband and I can be honest, gracious, understanding, and humorous at times. Although marriage can definitely be challenging, I've learned that two simple things benefit my marriage greatly: grace and a sense of humor.

We're all fighting a daily battle against to-do lists and responsibilities that pull us this way and that. Extending grace to our spouse means seeing him through the gospel. We are all imperfect, yet Jesus loves us more than we could ever imagine. Though we are undeserving of His love, He moved toward us in humility, gentleness, patience, and forgiveness. We can give our spouse that same kind of love—the love of Jesus.

And the truth is, sometimes we just have to laugh. Take a deep breath. When my husband asked me what was for dinner, I could have had a meltdown. Tears were just below the surface. But because he lost it in a fit of laughter, the whole mood lightened, which helped bring down the walls I was beginning to put up to protect myself. Humor enables us to minimize what's truly insignificant.

How many conflicts could be easily resolved if we would just step back and give each other the gift of love and laughter? Our spouse is not our enemy. In Christ, we have been joined together to live with each other, for each other, and for the glory of God.

Lord, thank You for not treating me as my sins deserve. You have been patient, gracious, and forgiving toward me. Empower me to show the same kind of love You have shown me to my spouse and family. In Jesus' name, Amen.

- What offenses, annoyances, or differences do you need to overlook?
- Why do laughter or humor lighten the load of marriage and family for you?

One Holy Hand

Karen

The Lord *answered Moses, "Go out in front of the people. Take with you some of the elders of Israel and take in your hand the staff with which you struck the Nile, and go."*

—Exodus 17:5

"If only I had another set of hands!" It's the melodramatic lament of every mom, right? We can walk into the house carrying twelve library books in one hand, two backpacks in the other, with a diaper bag dragging in the wake of our desperation only to find—wait for it—the house a mess.

In moments like these, many of us have thought that if we just had more appendages, *then* we'd be fully equipped. Yes, then maybe we'd be able to take care of everybody and everything. Until then, we'll all just have to settle for messiness, madness, and *meh* because motherhood is just too much!

Have you been there? Me too. However, we can't stay there. Sometimes we have to mom-up and face the truth—even when the children, dishes, laundry, and dinner preparations are vying for our attention. We need to know this: the blood of Christ is enough.

Moses was leading the entire tribe of Israel through the desert, and he had to deal with some bristling personalities. To make matters worse, people were begging him to give them something he didn't have—water in the desert. Can you relate?

When you're feeling overwhelmed, here's what you can do: remind yourself of God's faithfulness. For Moses, his reminder was the staff he used to perform God's miracles. What God did through him before, God could do through him again.

Even if your current situation is unprecedented, delicately intricate, or severely exhausting, God wants you to grasp the most powerful reminder of all. God wants you to remember the perspective-changing aspect of the blood.

See, God could have reminded Moses of his staff that turned into a snake or parted the Red Sea (Exodus 4:3; 7:10, 12; 14:16). Instead, God reminded Moses of the staff "with which [he] struck the Nile" and turned the water to blood (Exodus 7:20). Jesus hadn't arrived on the scene yet, but the Old Testament was pointing toward the importance of the blood.

When Moses asked God what to do about having no water in the desert, He answered, "Go out in front of the people. Take with you some of the elders of Israel and take in your hand the staff with which you struck the Nile, and go" (Exodus 17:5).

One holy hand and a reminder of the blood will always be enough.

What's in your hand? The vacuum handle, car keys, an odd sock, or tear-soaked tissues? Hold on to God's faithfulness. You don't need more hands, mama. As God helped you before, He can help you again.

Dear heavenly Father, I know that You "open your hand and satisfy the desires of every living thing" (Psalm 145:16). Give me the strength to take care of my household just as You gave Moses the strength to take care of the Israelites. In Jesus' name, Amen.

- Think about your hands today. What will you put in them? List a few of these tasks.
- What will be your prayer for those activities?

- What is the connection between Jesus' sacrifice and the work you do with your hands?

Dreaming Big

Ruth

Jesus said to Simon, "Don't be afraid; from now on you will fish for people." So they pulled their boats up on shore, left everything and followed him.

—Luke 5:10–11

We were just finishing dinner when my husband and I started asking our kids what they wanted to be when they grew up. If you have ever done the same with your kids, you know the answers are never predictable!

I looked at our youngest daughter, Sophia, and asked, "What about you?" Energized by the countless opportunities, she paused and then finally said, "A ballerina and a singer."

Kids love to dream, don't they? It didn't bother Sophia one bit that she has never taken a ballet lesson. She had made up her mind. She wanted to dance!

Full of imagination, and lacking the awareness of all the real-life obstacles, children love to dream. Dreaming comes easily. Dreaming is fun. And the possibility of fulfilling a dream actually seems realistic.

You know as well as I do, the older we get, the harder it is to dream. It's more challenging to believe, to trust, to risk, and to think beyond our own limitations. We settle in and get comfortable, play it safe, and forget to entertain the impossible.

When Jesus met His first disciples along the Sea of Galilee, He invited them on an adventure. He was leading them out of the ordinary.

They were used to casting nets and pulling in fish. The work wasn't easy, but it was familiar. And then Jesus showed up and asked them to dream, to envision a different future, to undertake a more risky endeavor.

Leave your nets. Leave your boats. Leave your tax collector booth. Leave your family. And go do something you never thought of doing or something you have no experience doing. Dream.

Follow Me, and I will make you fish for people.

Jesus was telling them to drop what they were doing in order to catch people. Every dream from God involves influencing others for Him. Our dreams are not just what we want to do, but ultimately about what God wants us to do. Go influence people—even if it seems impossible. Dream big.

As a family, we love to ask our kids what they want to be when they grow up, but we also ask God what He wants them to do. As moms, we can help our kids dream. Let's make our homes safe places to dream big and learn to trust that God will—and does—do the impossible through our simple acts of obedience.

Father, teach me to be a mom who believes You. Give me faith to step outside of what is comfortable and predictable. And help me encourage my children to do the same. Give them dreams to do big things for You. Raise them up in their generation to stand for Your name. In Jesus' name, Amen.

- Why (or why not) would you consider your home a safe place to dream?
- What might you do to encourage your kids to have a big vision for their lives?
- What is the difference between *dreaming* and *dreaming for God*?

The Dangerous Familiar

Karen

Formerly, when you did not know God, you were slaves to those who by nature are not gods. But now that you know God—or rather are known by God—how is it that you are turning back to those weak and miserable forces? Do you wish to be enslaved by them all over again?

—Galatians 4:8–9

"Aw, come on Mom and Dad . . . pleeeeease!" our kids begged when they spied a Free Kittens sign. My husband and I caved in and consented.

Our youngest, Spencer, chose a tiger kitten and proudly toted him out of the barn. When he placed the timid fur ball in the car, the kitten frantically dug his claws into Spencer, who let out a scream and let go of the cat. He scurried under the driver's seat, crawled up near the clutch, and somehow managed to squeeze through a small opening into the dashboard where we couldn't see him.

As an employee of an automaker, my husband assured us the kitty would be safe on the drive home. When we parked the car in the garage, the kitten still wouldn't come out. We opened the driver's door and tried to bribe our furry friend with milk and food. Surely the little kitty would get hungry and come out. And he did—a full two days later.

We promptly named him Dash. And we noticed something about him: whenever he wanted to escape, he would crawl up under the engine of our van and sleep. When we'd start the engine, he would dash out and run into the woods. When he wanted to escape the family frenzy for some alone time, he went back to what felt familiar even though it was connected to a horrible experience.

Sometimes we make the same kinds of choices. We revert back to a not-so-healthy habit because it feels familiar. Our hidden habits entice us to participate just a little. They promise to offer us rest and a feeling of familiarity, but in reality those habits are dangerous places for us to lodge.

Consider Paul's perspective: "Formerly, when you did not know God, you were slaves to those who by nature are not gods. But now that you know God—or rather are known by God—how is it that you are turning back to those weak and miserable forces? Do you wish to be enslaved by them all over again?" (Galatians 4:8–9). And that's just what returning to old, sinful habits makes us: weak and miserable.

Let's race to God instead of running back to our old ways. His Word is alive and active. It can help us break horrible habits and form new, Jesus-pleasing ones as we refuse to return to the dangerous familiar.

Dear Lord, forgive me for running to the familiar instead of to You. Break sin's hold on me as I strive to break old habits for Your glory. In Jesus' name, Amen.

- What destructive habit or sin trips you up again and again?
- Will you determine today to stop hiding out in old, destructive habits? Ask God to help you live in the light of His glorious grace and learn a new method of coping.

Is Mom Crabby *Again*?

Ruth

Rejoice in the Lord always. I will say it again: Rejoice!

—PHILIPPIANS 4:4

Not surprisingly, one Sunday morning my kids and I were running just a wee bit late for church. Honestly, it never fails: no matter what time we wake up, we end up scurrying around the house, and my unrealistic expectation of getting four small children ready without a glitch never seems to pan out.

This particular time I also made a dreadful mistake upon waking up. I chose to start getting ready *before* having my cup of coffee. And because my pastor-husband was already at church, getting four kids dressed, fed, brushed, combed, presentable, and happy fell to me. Not that I mind, but doing all that *before* a cup of coffee? Let's just say that isn't a wise choice.

We rushed out the door, and while backing out of the garage, I announced to my four children, "Um, I'm really frustrated right now. No one can seem to get ready in time—ever! And, well, I just want everyone to know that I did *not* have my coffee this morning."

My kids—ages ten, eight, six, and four at the time—did not have to guess: Mom was crabby . . . again!

Now, this really wasn't about a cup of coffee or running out of time to get ready. It had everything to do with my inability to control my emotions in the midst of a chaotic situation.

The truth is, our attitude sets the tone for our families, homes, and marriages. It can be especially difficult to rejoice in our day when we're feeling overwhelmed by all that comes with motherhood. But we must remember that our children are watching. Instead of contributing to a crabby environment like I did that Sunday morning, how about one filled with joy even in the midst of chaos?

Lord, help me to find my joy in You. Teach me to rejoice in what I have that I don't deserve instead of complaining about the things that don't seem to go right in my day. You have blessed me in every way through Christ. Fill me with Your Spirit today so that I may experience real and lasting joy in You. In Jesus' name, Amen.

- In what area of your life are you most struggling to find joy right now? Marriage? Parenting? Friendship? Work? Something else?
- How does rejoicing help you overcome complaining or crabbiness?

Befriending the Bitter

Karen

"Don't call me Naomi," she told them. "Call me Mara, because the Almighty has made my life very bitter."

—RUTH 1:20

Have you ever heard someone say, "Surround yourself with positive people"? It's great to have sunshiny sisters in your life. Laughter, smiles, encouragement, and creativity abound. Who doesn't enjoy busting a gut with the besties?

There's nothing wrong with having friends who exude the joy of the Lord. But I just wonder, if we don't make friends with the unpleasant personalities in our midst, what will become of them? We might feel delightful when we're with friendly ladies, but is it the sweet souls or the bitter who need more sugar? Who is willing to stand next to the Maras?

What, you don't have any "Maras" in your life? You do; they're just the Naomis who went through bad times and haven't bounced back.

Naomi means "pleasant." *Mara* means "bitter." In Ruth 1:20, Naomi asked all her old acquaintances to stop calling her the name that meant pleasant and to instead call her Mara. In order to see the context of Ruth 1:20, let's look at this portion of Scripture with the verses before and after.

"So the two women went on until they came to Bethlehem. When they arrived in Bethlehem, the whole town was stirred because of them, and the women exclaimed, 'Can this be Naomi?'"

"Don't call me Naomi," she told them. "Call me Mara, because the Almighty has made my life very bitter. I went away full, but the LORD has brought me back empty. Why call me Naomi? The LORD has afflicted me; the Almighty has brought misfortune upon me." So Naomi returned from Moab accompanied by Ruth" (Ruth 1:19–22).

This was big. The entire city of Bethlehem was talking about Naomi coming home! There was cause for celebration, tears of joy, and stories about the "good old days." Bethlehem's pleasant sister was back!

Except she wasn't pleasant anymore. She was still mourning her devastating loss. She couldn't get out of her despair even for such a momentous occasion.

And Ruth stayed by her side.

Do you know anyone who has experienced a huge loss but hasn't moved on? Perhaps she needs a steadfast friend.

It takes a lot of energy to be the Ruth in someone's life. Maras can soak a sister dry. If we see it that way, it will be that way. But if we see ourselves as ministers of the sweet riches of Christ, then we can invest time and befriend the bitter. They need the sugar of a stable sister who won't walk away.

Dear heavenly Father, let me be a steady friend who doesn't rush anyone through the grieving process. In Jesus' name, Amen.

→ Is there someone you know who has become embittered by life's circumstances? What will you do today to reach out to her?

___

___

___

___

Rest Time

Ruth

God blessed the seventh day and made it holy, because on it he rested from all the work of creating that he had done.

—Genesis 2:3

Taking a break from all of the to-dos isn't something most moms do easily.

I sat on the couch just to take a break after a busy day at home. Feeling a bit worn-out from taking care of the kids, refilling drinks, answering endless questions, and trying to keep the house from burning down, I needed some rest!

Within minutes, out of the large picture windows on the eastern side of our house, I could see my husband's car. Just over the small hill about a block away, I saw him pulling onto our street—almost home.

I immediately jumped up.

I was sure that if he walked in after a busy day at work and I was sitting on the couch, he would think I had done nothing all day. I had to look busy. All the time. After this scenario played out multiple times over several months, I finally came to my senses.

What on earth was I doing?!

I decided to ask my hubby what his thoughts would be if he walked in and I were sitting on the couch. He looked at me like I was a little crazy and assured me that he wouldn't think anything about it. *What?!* For all those months my own faulty thinking had tricked me into believing I couldn't rest, not even for a minute.

Rest is a difficult concept, especially for those of us living in a Western culture that places high value on action. We quietly feel condemned or ashamed when we're doing nothing. Some of us are afraid to sit, relax, unwind, or do nothing for too long. We have this imaginary voice telling us, "Get up; do something. There's work to be done. Don't rest. There is too much to do!"

But when I read the Bible, I see multiple examples of Jesus resting. He often got away from the masses. He snuck away to quiet places. He rested.

I have come to understand that the only way to pour out the best of who I am to my family and in my ministry is to *sloooow* down. Make time for the moments of life. Be still. Settle my soul. And just relax.

The housework? It will still be there tomorrow.

Father, help me to find my rest in You. Be my strength. Quiet my soul. In all that I have to do as a mom, give me rest. Enable to me to relax, knowing that my life is found in You. In Jesus' name, Amen.

- When have you felt guilty for wanting to relax?
- Why do you find it difficult to slow down and rest?
- How can you make time for rest?

Let Them Hear So They Can See

Karen

How, then, can they call on the one they have not believed in? And how can they believe in the one of whom they have not heard? And how can they hear without someone preaching to them?

—Romans 10:14

How do you take compliments? When someone comments on something you've done, or on your new hairstyle or tasty casserole, what do you do? Do you find it uncomfortable and start to mumble, "Oh, no. It was nothing. It's not really that good," thereby diminishing the praise because it makes you feel a bit awkward?

Receiving praise, compliments, and words of affirmation is often difficult for people. I really dislike getting complimented to my face. Normally the talkative type, I suddenly find myself at a loss for words. On one hand, I don't want to look like I'm a braggart. However, on the other hand, I know it kind of takes the wind out of the other person's sails when I try to tell them that they have it all wrong, that what I did wasn't really all that great. This response creates social awkwardness too.

So what's a gal to do? We are to deflect the praise to God, giving Him the credit and glory.

I have found that when I intentionally point the praise aimed at me toward Christ instead, I feel less awkward. And it serves an even greater purpose: those who are watching me hear about the love of God. Best of all, I'm able to share Christ without sounding preachy.

I first became interested in having a relationship with Christ when I observed a woman who did this exact thing. She was an excellent cook, a devoted wife, and a loving mother. People were drawn to her by her genuine concern and bubbly personality. But whenever I complimented her—on the way she dealt with people or her yummy homemade brownies—she somehow always brought God into the picture. She would say how much she appreciated God's provision in her life, so she was happy to share her brownies with others. Or she would mention how grateful she was that God enabled her to have children, so she found pure enjoyment in caring for them. Whenever I pointed out something I loved about her, she continually pointed me to God.

Adopting such a habit in our own lives can help to carry out the command in Romans 10:14. We don't need a pulpit or a platform to share Christ with others. Sometimes we can simply do it with how we respond to a sincere compliment from someone in our everyday lives. When others hear us honor God, they see Him up close. When they spy us giving Him credit, they catch a glimpse of His glory.

So, the next time someone tosses a compliment your way, make it your aim to honor God with your gracious and humble reply.

Father, may I be humble when complimented, but may I also be ever mindful to give the credit and glory to You, pointing others to the salvation and wholeness You offer. In Jesus' name, Amen.

- On a scale of 1 to 10 (1 being *not good at all* and 10 being *great!*), how good are you at receiving a compliment?
- How does it challenge or change your thinking when you ponder deflecting praise directed your way toward God?

Skilled Living

Ruth

Be very careful, then, how you live—not as unwise, but as wise.

—Ephesians 5:15

I grew up in a family where both of my parents worked outside the home, and dinnertime was whenever we got around to it. My husband grew up in a home where his mom had dinner ready every night at exactly 5:00 p.m. You can imagine some of the conflicting ideas we had to work out during our first year of marriage!

Cooking, for instance, didn't come naturally to me. I was not born with the skill to cook—and for that matter, there are lots of other skills I didn't possess from birth. I had to learn to sing, I learned a certain set of skills to graduate from college, and I'm still learning what it looks like to be a God-honoring wife and mom.

To do most things in life, we have to intentionally learn how. We study something to become skilled.

When the Bible uses the word *wise*, it doesn't just mean intelligence. Wisdom in the Bible is not being smart; wisdom is skilled living. The word in Hebrew for *wisdom* is often translated as "skilled." So having wisdom, according to the Bible, is being able to understand and apply God's truth to our lives. We aren't born with wisdom or skill. We have to learn to be skilled at navigating the many life choices we face.

This is why the apostle Paul told us to "be very careful" how we live. There is a wise way and a foolish way to walk through life. As followers of Jesus, we are commanded to be wise, or skilled, in how we live.

Skilled in parenting.

Skilled in our thoughts.

Skilled in our marriage.

Skilled at controlling our emotions.

Skilled at how we use our time.

Skilled at using our gifts for others.

We aren't supposed to just wing it, attempting to get by or get through life. The good news is that the Holy Spirit is our Helper. As we set our hearts on trusting and following Jesus, we enter into the school of skilled living. Just as the Holy Spirit led and empowered Jesus, He will do the same for us.

The best way to learn how to be skilled at living is to follow Jesus' example. After all, He is the way, the truth, and the life (John 14:6).

Father, empower me through the Holy Spirit to live wisely. Help me to follow in Jesus' footsteps. He is the way, the truth, and the life. I want my life to be found in Him. Give me grace for the many times I fall short. In Jesus' name, Amen.

- In what areas of your life would you consider yourself unskilled, and why?
- In what area of your life do you need to more closely follow Jesus' example?

Playing Favorites

Karen

Jacob said to Rebekah his mother, "But my brother Esau is a hairy man while I have smooth skin. What if my father touches me? I would appear to be tricking him and would bring down a curse on myself rather than a blessing." His mother said to him, "My son, let the curse fall on me. Just do what I say; go and get them for me."

—Genesis 27:11–13

Parenting 101 offers many unspoken and logical rules. Don't, for example, reward a two-year-old's temper tantrum by giving her the new toy she's screaming for. Don't let a short-on-sleep child skip a much-needed nap on the day of an evening event where he needs to be on his best behavior. And—probably one of the classics—when it comes to your children, do *not* play favorites. It never ends well.

There's a mom in the Old Testament who broke that last parental rule of thumb. She not only favored one child over the other, but she also allowed her preferential attitude to lead to unscrupulous actions. The resulting familial turmoil not only affected her immediate family but had ramifications for generations.

Rebekah was the wife of Isaac. She and the Mister had twin boys, Esau and Jacob. Esau was the first twin to emerge from the womb, but Jacob became Rebekah's favorite. When the boys grew older, Jacob—on a day Esau was particularly hungry—duped his big brother into selling his birthright for a simple bowl of lentil stew.

Later, when their father lay dying with his eyesight nearly gone,

Rebekah helped Jacob steal yet again. She plotted with him to deceive Isaac into pronouncing a blessing over Jacob instead of over Esau, thereby snatching the blessing intended for the firstborn. Rachel put goatskins on Jacob's hands and neck to disguise him as Esau, who had hairy skin rather than Jacob's smooth skin. When Isaac felt it, he blessed Jacob, assuming it was really Esau. Rebekah's deception caused enmity between the brothers that continued for years.

Although we as moms know we shouldn't play favorites, if we're honest, we will admit that sometimes it's hard not to. We may get along better with one of our children than the others. Or we share common interests and passions with one. Perhaps more common is this scenario: one of our children is so much like us that we see in them what we don't like about ourselves, and it drives us absolutely nuts, causing us to gravitate instead toward a child with a different personality. That has surely been the case with me!

Let's resist being a Rebekah; let's refuse to play favorites. If we're prayerful and careful as we mother our children, God can impart to us a love for each of our children that is special and unique without being preferential. We won't be playing favorites. Instead, we'll be loving profusely—and saving ourselves and our descendants from strife and turmoil as well.

Father, forgive me for the times I have treated one child better than another. May You, as the Source of all love, help me love each of my children abundantly. In Jesus' name, Amen.

- Describe a time when you were tempted to play favorites with your children. Did you give into this temptation? If so, what happened?

- What factors draw you more to one child than another? Take this situation to God today, asking Him to help you lavishly love all of your children.

Praying for Your Husband

Ruth

"My prayer is not for them alone. I pray also for those who will believe in me through their message, that all of them may be one, Father, just as you are in me and I am in you. May they also be in us so that the world may believe that you have sent me."

—John 17:20–21

As hard as motherhood can be, being a father and husband is no cakewalk either. And so I'm learning to pray—or pray more often—for my husband.

I pray for his heart, his integrity, and his faith. The pressures of serving in ministry, providing for our family, and making the many decisions I know he faces all day long are on my prayer list too.

I pray because I know there are some things only God can do for him. Prayer is a way I surrender him to the Lord's provision and protection. For as much as I can do for my husband and with him, there are some things too big and beyond my control. And so I pray often for him.

When Jesus prayed for His disciples, He prayed they would be one. He asked the Father to keep them united. He knew the disciples would encounter obstacles, opposition, temptations, and trials. His prayer was that there would be a strength in their relationship that would ultimately point back to God.

Prayer is offering our hearts to our Father and asking Him to protect our marriage. It's taking the real threats to our unity and asking our Father to bind us together, keeping us strong.

In what ways do you need to begin praying for your husband? How can you take what's out of your control and surrender it to your Father? Jesus had to teach His disciples how to pray because, honestly, sometimes we either don't pray at all or we pray for the wrong things.

So today, regardless of what is going on, begin to pray for your husband. Pray hard and pray often. Ask your Father to lead your husband, provide for him, protect him, and draw him close to Jesus. One of the greatest acts of love for our husband is to lift him before the throne of God.

Father, I lift up my husband to You. Would You pour out Your Spirit on him today? Give him grace. Empower him with Your strength and wisdom. Guard him from the evil one, and enable him to walk in faithfulness to You. I pray that You would surround our marriage, protecting the unity and intimacy we have. Use our marriage to glorify You. In Jesus' name, Amen.

- How have you seen prayer change your own heart?
- What Scriptures could you begin to pray for or over your husband?

____

____

____

____

____

Junk-Closet Heart

Karen

Who perceives his unintentional sins? Cleanse me from my hidden faults.

—Psalm 19:12 HCSB

Our basement furnace room is not a pretty sight right now. This out-of-the-way space is a catchall place for off-season items and assorted memorabilia. To combat clutter and keep objects organized, over the years we've purchased shelves and large plastic totes to neatly store our family's stuff.

In my perfect plan, bins are labeled, shelves are stocked tidily with homemade canned goods, and holiday decorations are nestled neatly in our oh-so-organized furnace storage room. And, truthfully, this is how it usually goes.

Well, 82 percent of the time.

However, when we aren't intentional to actually walk into the room and place items in the proper bin or situate them on their designated shelf, we tend to revert to the open, drop, and shut method of organization: open the door, drop the item just inside the room, and shut the door tightly so the accumulating pile of clutter is not visible from the adjacent family rec room.

The result is an unattractive pile of stuff that slowly grows and messes with my plan for an orderly storage room. When this occurs, I have to stop what I'm doing and carve out time to sort the items and put them back in their proper places.

At times my heart can become a catchall for clutter and junk too. It is not my intent to have a messed-up heart that harbors incorrect attitudes or contaminated thoughts that eventually might lead to wrong actions or unconfessed sin.

However, when I'm not intentional about putting those thoughts and feelings in their proper place—under the authority of Christ—they can soon breed a bunch of unwanted and sinful stuff in my spirit that messes with God's plan for me to behave like Jesus. And although the outside world may not see it, behind the door of my heart I know the junk pile is there.

For believers to keep this spiritual clutter at bay, we must make a regular habit of asking God to show us if we are collecting unwanted attitudes, thoughts, and issues. Are we harboring anger, bitterness, envy, or ill will? Have we accumulated spiritual laziness or a love for something that is greater than our love for God?

Without putting these away by confessing them to God, we might end up with an unintentional pile of spiritual junk that often can lead to sins we never set out to commit. Hidden anger in our heart toward another becomes harshly hurled words. Secret envy morphs into gossip. Behind-the-scenes bitterness begets openly bad behavior.

Let's make Psalm 19:12 our heart-cleaning plea: "Who perceives his unintentional sins? Cleanse me from my hidden faults" (HCSB). God is the master Declutterer who alone can help us deal with the messes we make.

Let's allow Him to clean out the clutter of our hearts and make our spirits whole again. This is spiritual pile-busting at its very best.

Dear Lord, teach me to bring any unconfessed sins to You early so they don't pile up and make a mess of my heart. I want to become more like Your Son each day. In Jesus' name, Amen.

- Could your heart use a good decluttering? List any spiritual junk you've allowed to accumulate.
- In what ways does Psalm 19:12 help you to clear away the rubbish?

Involving Your Children in Ministry

Ruth

Serve wholeheartedly, as if you were serving the Lord, not people.

—Ephesians 6:7

Several years ago, our family was sitting around the dinner table. It was late December and, typical for northwest Ohio, the weather was cold and snowy. We were expecting several inches of additional snow that night.

My husband and I had been discussing friends of ours who were not Christians. They had a large family and were struggling with the costs of clothing, transportation, and education. Their children were around the same ages as ours, and on numerous occasions we had been to their house.

As we talked and our concern for them grew, one of our kids asked, "What can we do for them?" For the next ten to fifteen minutes, we brainstormed ways we could help this family and show them the love of Christ. Finally, we landed on a gift card for gas money. At this conclusion, we sprang into action!

Did I mention it was snowing, *really* snowing?

And so we shoveled a path out of our driveway, climbed into the van, and headed toward their house with this surprise. The plan was to place the card and money inside their front storm door, ring the bell so they would find the gift, and then race to the car.

Our kids were like ninjas, hiding behind bushes and a car, then making sure the gift was firmly secured in their door. I wouldn't say they were as quiet as they should have been, especially when they rang the doorbell! Fortunately—and most importantly—they made it back to the van without being spotted. Still to this day they talk about that night.

The thrill of secretly surprising someone.

The adventure.

The challenge.

The snow.

And especially the joy of getting to be the hands and feet of Jesus and the memory of doing it all as a family. This act of kindness left a lasting impression on our kids' hearts and in their minds.

Motherhood is busy. It's full of unexpected and exhausting moments. It's not always possible to do what you did before having kids. This season is just that—a season. But motherhood doesn't have to mean leaving behind ministry or no longer living on mission for Jesus.

Ministry can happen in all sorts of ways. God wants to use you right where you are and with those whom He has entrusted to you. Doing ministry, loving those around you, and serving those in need can leave a lasting impression on your kids.

Don't forget that passing on faith is not just what we say, but it's also what we do—together!

Father, give me eyes to see those around us who are in need. Help me to see motherhood as an opportunity to do ministry, even if it looks different. Give us opportunities to serve and love those around us together. We want to be a family who lives to glorify You in all we do. In Jesus' name, Amen.

- In what ways has motherhood changed how you do ministry?
- What new doors for ministry has motherhood opened for you?

- What are ways you can involve your children in loving and serving those around you?

Tethered or Tattered?

Karen

The Lord *is my strength and my [impenetrable] shield; My heart trusts [with unwavering confidence] in Him, and I am helped; Therefore my heart greatly rejoices, And with my song I shall thank Him and praise Him.*

—Psalm 28:7 AMP

My heart is such a fickle little thing. It just can't seem to make up its mind. One moment it is content and calm—until I receive an e-mail from someone who is upset with me. Then my heart begins to fray from the stress.

Sometimes my heart is smiling and confident. Then my child makes a bad choice—a really bad choice. My hopeful heart becomes fearful and anxious. I'm not only disappointed in my child; I'm also concerned about what my child's wrong choice might do to my reputation as a mother.

A few days later my back-and-forth heart seems settled and serene. Then I hear the words *terminal cancer.* My heart unravels at the difficult news that a family member must process.

The shrapnel that flies when I receive disturbing or discouraging news leaves my heart in pieces. And my tattered heart overtakes my emotions and affects my ability to carry out even simple, daily tasks. Try as I might, I just can't focus. My mind wanders, and my heart flutters with fright.

Is there a remedy for a tattered heart? Or are we destined to live with ragged emotions that threaten to steal our peace?

During those times when we're certain our hearts can't take any more, Psalm 28:7 urges us to surrender those emotions to God. He is our strength. Our shield. We can trust in Him. And trust means relying on and confidently leaning on Him to find our help. What will the result be? The caboose of the verse tells us: "Therefore my heart greatly rejoices, And with my song I shall thank Him and praise Him" (AMP).

We can have a joyful heart—one that praises God no matter our lot in life. But first we need to go to Him for strength.

Reminding ourselves of God's power is important. He created the world. He is in the sound of thunder and the flash of lightning. He can uproot mountains and command the seas. Why, oh why, do we think He can't handle our day-to-day problems?

As we tether our heart to God's truth, we can keep our heart from becoming tattered. A tethered heart rests securely, knowing God is our strength and shield. He will restore our joy and enable us to sing His praise.

Will you join me today in tethering your heart to God's Word? Read it. Soak it in. Speak it out loud. Write it on the sticky note of your heart.

Dear Lord, help me each day to let Your love secure my unsettled soul, keeping my heart tethered to You and preventing it from becoming tattered as I soak in the wonder of Your holy and powerful Word. In Jesus' name, Amen.

- Do you find your heart bouncing back and forth between trust and panic?
- How can Psalm 28:7 help tether your heart to God and His Word?

Teaching Your Children Courage

Ruth

Finally, be strong in the Lord and in his mighty power.

—EPHESIANS 6:10

A few years ago, one of my children woke up in the middle of the night, wide-eyed and trembling with fright. She didn't know why she was afraid; she just was. She has always been fearful at night, but this night she was terrified.

No matter what I said, she couldn't comprehend what I was saying. I found myself raising my voice louder trying to reason with her. Finally, I realized that she didn't need me to scold her or give her reasons *not* to be afraid. She just needed me to hold her. And that's what I did. After five minutes, I prayed with her, and she let out a deep sigh of relief.

As moms, we do everything we can to protect and even prevent our children from having a reason to fear, but how do we help prepare our children for difficult times?

This is what God did when He sent Joshua to lead the Israelites:

> Be strong and courageous, because you will lead these people to inherit the land I swore to their ancestors to give them. Be strong and very courageous. Be careful to obey all the law my servant Moses gave you; do not turn from it to the right or to the left, that you may be successful wherever you go. Keep this Book of the Law always on your lips; meditate on it day and night, so that you may be careful to do everything written in it. Then you will be prosperous and successful.

> Have I not commanded you? Be strong and courageous. Do not be afraid, do not be discouraged, for the LORD your God will be with you wherever you go. (Joshua 1:6–9)

God was standing beside Joshua, cheering him on. When every circumstance seemed against him, God told him to be strong and courageous! Be strong and very courageous! Be strong and courageous! He was preparing Joshua with the truth of His Word and His promises.

This command may seem simple to you, but I think it can be life-changing for our children.

Let's be honest. We all need the reminder that God is more powerful than we are. I have had to whisper those words, "Be strong and courageous," to myself in dark moments of despair to remind myself that He is with me.

But that strength isn't our own, is it? It's the strength and power that God provides. In Christ, we have all that we need to stand firm and stay strong. So more than preparing our children to be strong on their own, we need to prepare our children to be strong in the Lord!

Father, give me Your strength. Protect me from worry and anxiety. Help me prepare my own children to stand firm in You. By the power of Your Spirit, give them courage so that they can stand for You in their generation. In Jesus' name, Amen.

- What is the difference between teaching your children to be courageous and teaching them to be strong in the Lord?
- What can you do to prepare your children to be "strong and courageous"?
- How can you model for your children trusting God even in trials?

Being Right Doesn't Give You the Right

Karen

Whoever loves a quarrel loves sin.

—Proverbs 17:19

I just love to have the last word. Especially in my marriage.

And my insistence on being the last one to speak is fueled by my desire to be "right." I not only want to be *right*; I want to make sure that my husband knows that he's *wrong*! Because I have a great memory—and my husband does not—this can be a setup for marital conflict. The poor guy just can't win. I push and push and insist I know how something went down. He feels trapped and just wants us to drop it already.

But people who love to be right *never* want to drop it. That takes all the fun away! And, yes, we somehow think it's fun to verbally back someone into a corner with our "I am right and I *will* have the last word" mind-set.

Oh, sisters, this should not be!

Proverbs 17:19 says, without giving us any wiggle room, "Whoever loves a quarrel loves sin."

Double ouch!

This verse sure slaps me upside my stubborn head. A good verbal joust is something I rather enjoy. My flesh eats up the feeling of being right and having the last word. But then I see this Scripture staring me in the face, telling me that a person who loves quarreling actually loves to sin. Oh my! I don't want to love sin. Seeing it put this way snaps my soul to attention in the most serious of ways.

So, what are we last-word-and-always-right people to do? We must be mindful of the flaws in our own strengths. You see, many strengths, carried to extremes, can become weaknesses. Some of us have good memories. Some of us are verbally articulate. Some of us place a high value on truth and accuracy. However, any of these strengths can become a weakness when we also mix in a little of our flesh—the part of us that loves to quarrel.

Let's guard our strengths and not let them morph into weaknesses—especially when it comes to a verbal exchange that might escalate into an all-out quarrel.

The next time we want to be right—and to have the last word—let's remember God's word to us in Proverbs 17:19 and stop a brawl before it even starts.

Father, please gently remind me, when I feel the desire to argue welling up inside of me, that I need to love Your Word and hate sin. Please keep my lips from quarrelling. In Jesus' name, Amen.

- Have you ever thought before about the concept of loving a quarrel being the same as loving sin? How will this scriptural truth change how you interact with others today?
- Is there one person in particular this brings to mind? How will you speak differently with him or her the next time you converse?

Opening Your Home

Ruth

Offer hospitality to one another without grumbling.

—1 Peter 4:9

I had it all planned out. We would celebrate Easter dinner at our house with some of the families from our church staff. Because we all lived a few hours from family, it was easiest for us to celebrate together. So I got busy planning what I thought would be the perfect day.

I had planned for at least month. We would have an egg hunt in the backyard that the kids would love. I envisioned them running, laughing, and exploring. Meanwhile, the perfect meal would be waiting for us all when the hunt was over. I was sure this was going to be a wingdinger of a day fellowshipping with our friends.

And then reality set in—with perfect timing, of course.

Two days before the perfectly planned get-together, when everything had been purchased and prepared, our daughter Sophia got croup. And there went our Easter plans. Before it even got off the ground, our attempt at hospitality came crashing down!

It seems like time and time again our planned hospitality is foiled by the unexpected incidents that come with family life.

But, let's be honest, this isn't the only threat to hospitality. It isn't always the fault of one of our children. Sometimes we don't invite others in because we're too busy, too concerned about the condition of our home, or just uninterested in investing in others. Practicing hospitality isn't always easy.

The word *hospitality* means being generous to guests. Making room for friends. Carving out time and space for them to belong. Opening our home and opening our heart. It's sharing a meal, having coffee, making tea, or making a fire. Hospitality is the command to be others-centered with our home.

It's easy in these busy years of motherhood to lose sight of the value of welcoming others in and cultivating meaningful relationships. It requires seeing our home and our space as a place to minister to others—just how God intended it to be.

Father, help me to see my home as Your space. Give me eyes to see the value of inviting others in, giving them the best of who we are and what we have. Enable me to be generous with my time and my attention. I want our house to be a place where friends feel welcome and at home. In Jesus' name, Amen.

- Are you more inclined to offer hospitality or to wait for someone else to offer you hospitality? Why?
- Do you find it difficult to practice hospitality? If so, why?
- What do you see as the main reason you don't open your home to friends more often?

Within Earshot, Within Heartshot

Karen

About midnight Paul and Silas were praying and singing hymns to God, and the other prisoners were listening to them.

—Acts 16:25

Everyone has an opportunity to observe Jesus in us. There are some souls who are watching us closely and some souls who are only within earshot. We are afforded the honor of influence for moments or sometimes years. In our darkest times we may have the most attentive audience. Will we be sound asleep, sobbing bitterly, or praising God despite the pain?

Regardless of your feelings toward it, social media is such an interesting place. We have close friends whom we follow daily, and then we have distant acquaintances with whom we rarely make contact. It's surprising when we receive a message or a comment from someone in the "distant friend" category. We get this feeling like, *Oh, wow, I didn't know they were keeping up with me*. It's a sobering reminder that people who are distant observers can also be careful note-takers.

Paul and Silas were thrown in prison because they were Jews and "throwing [the] city into an uproar" (Acts 16:20). They were severely flogged and put in an inner cell in the prison. The jailer was told to "guard them carefully" (v. 23).

There were two sections of seating in this prison: those who were close enough to hear with their ears and the jailer who was ordered to watch the prisoners closely with his eyes. We have similar categories of onlookers: those whom God has purposely placed in close proximity and those who can only hear our hearts from a distance.

Paul and Silas, isolated and with their feet in chains, chose to sing. All those in the prison who were within earshot were now within "heartshot." When we have someone's ears, there's a chance we have his or her heart.

As Paul and Silas sang praises, the foundations of the prison were shaken by an earthquake. *Everyone's* chains came loose. All those within heartshot were now free. The jailer fell at Paul's and Silas's feet. He asked, "What must I do to be saved?" (v. 30).

The jailer knew they had the answer to his question about salvation.

Freedom came to those listening from a distance and to the man who was closely watching. On social media, are the close followers and distant drop-ins able to hear you singing a song of salvation? You never know when your worship will loosen their chains!

If you're within earshot, you're within heartshot. When a prisoner's heart is hearing, freedom is a salvation song away.

Dear heavenly Father, You allow me opportunities to display my faith every day. Let me be aware of my audience both near and far. I want to sing praises that draw others to You, the only One who can break a prisoner's chains. In Jesus' name, Amen.

- Think through your postings and interaction on social media. What are those who don't know Christ seeing and hearing on your posts?
- What questions can you ask yourself before posting that will help make sure you are pointing others to Jesus?

Becoming Less

Ruth

He must become greater and greater, and
I must become less and less.

—John 3:30 NLT

I didn't grow up in a Christian home. My parents were loving, supportive, and hardworking. I was also blessed to have grandparents who surrounded me with the same kind of love and support my parents gave me. But I didn't become a Christian until high school.

From an early age, I wondered about God. I had big questions. Scary questions. I would try to figure out what life was all about. By God's grace, a friend of mine invited me to youth group where I discovered God's love for me—and learned that life wasn't all about me. That's hard for a high school girl to accept!

Early in my Christian life, I wandered in and out of walking in God's truth. Like many Christians, I was asking God to follow me instead of the other way around.

On one occasion when I had been noticeably absent from youth group, my youth pastor sent me a note. The note contained a simple but powerful verse that God used to get my attention. It's a truth that God has buried deep in my heart: "He must become greater and greater, and I must become less and less" (NLT). John the Baptist spoke these words to remind his disciples that he came only to announce the Messiah, not *be* the Messiah.

John understood his place in God's plan. He had discovered that everything about his life and role was meant to point to the real Hero of the story—Jesus. John had to become less so that Jesus could become greater.

I'm guessing, if you're anything like me, you struggle with that. We all do! It's easy to want to be at the center of our universe. I can stay stuck in my own sin and selfishness, not allowing Jesus to show through in who I am and what I do. The greatness and glory of God get cloudy when I'm standing in the way.

As moms, we can be sure God is working His eternal purposes through us. In the middle of the hard stuff, mess, stress, and noise, God is at work. And He's saying to us today, *Become less, so I can become more!*

Father, thank You for saving me through Jesus' death on the cross. Thank You that I get to be a part of Your story. Enable me to become less so that You can become greater in me. May my kids see You through me. In Jesus' name, Amen.

- What are some examples of how you struggle with becoming less when God wants to become more?
- What are one or two things you can do in your family to become less so that Jesus can become more in you and in your home?

____

____

____

____

____

Domestic Detective Work

Karen

"In the morning, present yourselves tribe by tribe. The tribe the LORD chooses shall come forward clan by clan; the clan the LORD chooses shall come forward family by family; and the family the LORD chooses shall come forward man by man."

—JOSHUA 7:14

"Alright, who did it?" If there's a more ancient question in motherhood, I don't know what it is.

So much time is spent on motherhood mysteries. We spend so much time to find out who broke this, who hit whom, and who took another person's something-or-other. Domestic detective work is spiritually draining and emotionally exhausting.

First of all, we don't have time to hold court cases over every hijacked toy and scribble of toddler graffiti on the living room wall. Or over who left the bag of tortilla chips open after microwaving a plate of nachos. I don't want to be Judge Judy; I just want to be Mom Mommy. However, knowing the condition of our household and properly being able to diagnose the problems are integral parts of parenting.

In the Old Testament, Joshua led thousands of Israelites into various battles. The battle of Ai was one they lost. Joshua got on his face before the Lord to pray and ask why. God told him that there was sin among the people and that Joshua had to find out who was responsible.

God could've told Joshua who did it, but He didn't. Joshua had to go through the painstaking process of determining who was guilty. God wanted to give Joshua and the Israelites victory in battle, but God cared more about His children's hearts.

God cares about *our* children's hearts too. We need to probe, prove, and purge just as Joshua did. We need to ask God for wisdom as we address sin in our children's lives. (This, of course, needs to be handled delicately and with great discernment.)

The purging that happened in the Old Testament is hard for us to imagine and extremely severe, but the point we shouldn't miss is that God never wants lingering sin. The most important thing we moms can do is help our precious children recognize impurities in their hearts.

Jesus Christ is the only One who can truly wash away our children's sins, just like He washed away ours. We can't possibly do the work of the Holy Spirit in their lives, but we can love them, administer grace, and take the time to understand how they're really doing.

Domestic detective work will always be one of our duties. As we undertake the necessary investigation, may we help our children grow to be adults with pure hearts who have a passion to follow the Lord into all of life's battles.

Dear heavenly Father, let me seek You first to learn how to pursue the deeper matters of my children's hearts. I pray that I would love them enough to take the time to get to the root of their sin. Please give me wisdom and patience. I pray our family has hearts washed by Jesus. In Jesus' name, Amen.

- What are some recent opportunities you've had to be a domestic detective?
- How does the fact that God told Joshua to get to the bottom of who had sinned challenge or encourage you?

Nurturing Your Family

Ruth

Jesus went up on a mountainside and called to him those he wanted, and they came to him.

—Mark 3:13

Jesus often withdrew. He wasn't afraid to get away to be alone with God. He was certainly in demand: He had miracles to perform, crowds to teach, and a mission to accomplish. There was no shortage of things to do. Opportunities and demands pulled on Him from every side.

And yet He didn't neglect getting away to be with His Father and to nurture His disciples. Jesus got alone and got away to *give* of Himself—*all* of Himself. What a great model for us moms!

Mark 3:13 says Jesus "went up on a mountainside and called to him those he wanted." Who were those "he wanted"? They were His disciples, the ones He was building up and building into.

The pressing crowds and daunting mission were all teaching opportunities—on-the-job training. But Jesus knew He needed to carve out time just for His disciples. He needed a place where they could be alone, free from distractions.

In those moments, Jesus intentionally invested in those who would carry on His mission after He was gone. He did not neglect nurturing His disciples.

Jesus' example is an eye-opening reminder for us moms: sometimes we, too, need to pull back from opportunities, say no to invitations, and choose to give the best of who we are to our little disciples—our children.

Admittedly, a healthy balance isn't always easy to strike. With all of the demands and busyness, it's hard to say no. But we need to know that it's okay to say no to others so we can say yes to our family. As moms, we need to take a step back at times so we can give our best to our children, nurturing them with our time, attention, and gifts.

Maybe you're struggling to keep up with all that's expected of you. If so, perhaps one of the best things you can do right now is to say no! Is God calling you to pull back and make more space to nurture those who need you most right now? If so, don't be afraid. Don't feel guilty. Even Jesus knew how important it was to withdraw! He pulled back so that He could pour into the ones who needed Him most.

Father, give me wisdom to know when to say yes and when to say no. I want to give my best to You and to my family. Give me discernment about how I can better nurture my own children during this demanding season of life. In Jesus' name, Amen.

- Why can it be hard to say no?
- We need time to withdraw to nourish our soul and to nurture our children. How do you know when you are being too greedy with your own time?
- Are there areas where you sense God is calling you to pull back or say no right now?

Picking Up Dirty Socks (Again!)

Karen

She looks well to the ways of her household and
does not eat the bread of idleness.

—Proverbs 31:27 ESV

As a teen I loved hanging out at Miss Pat's house. Hands down, she made the best homemade noodles in the Midwest. Often you could find the creamy-white strips of flour, milk, and eggs drying on her kitchen counter, waiting to be tossed into a simmering pot of chicken soup. Or you might find a fresh fruit pie cooling near an open window, making her family eager for suppertime.

With as much energy as Miss Pat devoted to homemaking, you might think that was all she did. But it wasn't. She was also active outside her home. Among other things, Miss Pat volunteered at her kids' school, taught a weekly women's Bible study, and served as a youth group leader. Her love for Jesus was evident, and she introduced numerous teens and women to Christ, including me.

As busy as she was, Miss Pat reserved her greatest energy and most creative ideas for her first line of ministry: her own family and home. She modeled how to influence others for Christ not only with the words she spoke, but also with a heart of love that filled her home.

Sitting around her kitchen table, I learned Miss Pat's secret for getting things done. She had a method for doing laundry, a routine for her cleaning, a game plan for getting groceries, and a cheerful attitude while doing it all. Proverbs 31:27 tells us about a wife and mother who worked like this: "She looks well to the ways of her household and does not eat the bread of idleness" (ESV).

Now that I have my own home and family, these women inspire me, especially during those times when I find it easier to be idle rather than tackle work around the home. The snapshots of organized spaces and fabulous foods on my computer screen tempt me to spend hours peering at them rather than making them happen in my home.

When running my home seems overwhelming, I remember Miss Pat and the Proverbs 31 woman. Instead of hoping the house cleans itself or a hot meal materializes out of the computer, I'm learning to make a plan and get to work. It's helpful to keep the mind-set that caring for my home and family is a ministry.

This perspective helps me pick up socks and make dinner without resentment. It gives me strength when I've already put in a full day's work. While I'm doing these things for my family, I'm also doing them for God. What an honor it is to work for Him.

Dear Lord, teach me to look well to the ways of my household and not be idle, knowing it is actually You I'm serving. In Jesus' name, Amen.

- Ask yourself these important questions: *Am I laboring with a glad heart, or do I grumble about the tasks at hand? Do I view keeping a home as a duty and drudgery, or do I find it a privilege and pleasure?*
- How can Proverbs 31:27 help you gain a proper perspective?

Grow in Generosity

Ruth

Then he said to them, "Watch out! Be on your guard against all kinds of greed; life does not consist in an abundance of possessions."

—Luke 12:15

Isn't it interesting that Jesus had to say, "Watch out"?

As a baseball mom, I get the connection. With kids running around and only a modest net to keep balls from coming at us, attention is necessary. I often hear a shout of "heads up!" We never know if a foul ball is headed our way, so we duck and cover our heads. A foul ball is unexpected but always a possibility. It's certainly not enjoyable if you have to shield yourself from one! Watching out is a way to be on guard, stay alert, and keep your eyes open.

What's so interesting to me is that Jesus told us we need to do the same with greed. We need to "watch out" because unlike other sins, greed can be hard to spot. In fact, we don't have to have a lot of money to be greedy. Greed can land in the lap of the rich and the poor.

But what makes greed so dangerous is that it robs us of the life God wants for us. As our Provider, He's not against us having stuff, but He doesn't want the stuff to have us. Because when it does, greed cripples us and keeps us from being generous. This is the real danger of greed: living with tight fists instead of open hands.

Being generous can be tough because most times when we transition from marriage to family, finances become tighter. Expenses go up, and at times our ability to give goes down.

But let's not miss out on the blessings God has for us when we are generous.

When we live generously, joy is ours because we invest more in people than possessions. And isn't this the message of the gospel? We who were poor have become rich in Christ. He has done for us what we could never do for ourselves. God, who is rich in grace, has blessed us in every way through Christ.

We serve a generous Father who isn't stingy with His love. In response to His generosity, may we seek to grow in giving more. May we desire to give graciously to others in the same way God, in Christ, has given to us.

Father, thank You for being generous to me. You have blessed me far beyond what I deserve. Help me to invest more in people than in possessions. Show me ways I can bless others as a reflection of the ways You have blessed me. In Jesus' name, Amen.

- When have you been on the receiving end of someone else's generosity?
- What is the significance of Jesus saying, "Watch out"?
- What are ways you can begin modeling for your children a life of generosity?

Pick Me! Pick Me!

Karen

For we know, brothers and sisters, loved by God, that he has chosen you.

—1 THESSALONIANS 1:4

I stand with my back against the school's red brick wall, my woolen plaid skirt scratching my legs even though I have on my best cable-knit tights. Trying not to look desperate, I secretly pray I won't be the last one chosen for the team. It's recess time, and kickball is my classmates' game of choice. As I look at the captain pointing and choosing kids, my heart's cry is simple: "Pick me! Pick me!"

A few years later, I sit in sixth period awaiting the end-of-the-day announcement of the homecoming court nominees. Earlier that crisp autumn day, the lunchroom had been all abuzz, a whirlwind of scribbled ballots and nervous beauties seeking votes. Now that the folded papers are tallied and the results are being read, once again my heart's cry is, "Pick me! Pick me!"

College girls gather around the stately cement fountain in the middle of campus. It's the place where many women give others a glimpse of "the ring": the ring that means they are chosen and loved, soon to be some handsome young man's wife. While the ring finger on my left hand remains painfully naked, my heart's cry is still so very, very simple: "Will some man please pick me?"

Throughout much of my early life, I desired nothing more than to be wanted. Yet, at many points along the way, I felt rejection as someone else was chosen instead of me. It wasn't until late in college that a wonderful truth was shared with me: I am already chosen; I am already loved.

First Thessalonians 1:4 nails it: "For we know, brothers and sisters, loved by God, that he has chosen you."

We are loved by God. He's already picked us. So there's no need to hope and wish and cross our fingers for good luck. We won't be left standing against a wall, unloved and passed over for someone with more skill, better looks, or more brains. We are the objects of our Savior's love, and nothing we do will change His great love for us.

You are the one He's pointing at, in front of the whole wide world's schoolyard, boldly declaring both now and forever, *I choose you!*

Dear Lord, help me erase the negative thoughts that run through my mind at times, making me feel unloved and rejected. Remind me that I am chosen and dearly loved both now and forever. In Jesus' name, Amen.

→ Will you cling to the very words of God? Let them be louder than the voices from your past or the jeers of the present or even your own negative self-talk that tells you you're not worthy, not loved, not ________ enough. Fill in the blank, and then fill your mind with God's truth about you instead: you are loved!

Teaching Children to Pray

Ruth

Jesus said, "Let the little children come to me, and do not hinder them, for the kingdom of heaven belongs to such as these."

—MATTHEW 19:14

"Dear Lawd, I pray for my mommy and my daddy. I pray for Ginger [the hamster]. I pray You to help me sleep. I pray for all the sick people. Amen."

Sweet Sophia, barely four years old at the time, whispered this precious prayer. There's nothing flashy about a child's prayer. Yes, sometimes their prayers are silly, and sometimes they really don't make sense, but they always remind us of how God wants us to come to Him.

Honest. Innocent. Confident. Childlike.

Routinely in Jesus' ministry, He not only welcomed children, but He pointed to them as examples of kingdom life.

Children were an example of trust and lack of pretense (Matthew 18:2–5).

Jesus warned against leading children astray or causing them to sin (Matthew 18:6).

Jesus blessed children and taught that the kingdom belonged to those who have a childlike faith in Him (Matthew 19:13–15).

Children matter to Jesus, and as moms, we appreciate this truth. We have been given these precious little ones to steward, shape, train, and ultimately release one day.

There seems to be an overwhelming trend to start as young as possible with some sort of method or curriculum to help our kids connect with Jesus. I'm not suggesting there's anything wrong with using a certain study. Yes, of course we want our children to learn about God. But what if we started out simple? Really simple: with teaching them to pray.

After all, calling out to God is a person's first expression of faith. I think one of the most effective ways to teach children to pray is to let them pour their sweet hearts out to God. Like my Sophia, children can pray from a young age, and whether they are praying for pet hamsters or their siblings, God hears them.

Beginning when our children were very little, we have prayed with each of them individually every night before they go to bed. We ask them if there is anything they want to pray about. And we pray before meals. We pray when something comes up that we feel needs to be prayed about right at that moment.

If we teach our children to go to God when they are little, they just may carry that habit with them for life. We teach them to pray because getting older doesn't always mean getting stronger, and life is full of uncertainties and heartache. Regardless of age, we are powerless. And isn't that what prayer is really all about? We go to God in our neediness and poverty because we know that—in His abundance—He has all that we need.

Teaching our children to pray is showing them how to do life with God instead of doing it alone.

Father, thank You for loving me by listening to me. I praise You because You are with me. I am weak, but You are strong. Help my kids to trust and love You. Even now, when they are young, give them a heart that hungers for You. In Jesus' name, Amen.

- At what point in your walk with the Lord did you really start praying? Why then?

- Why is it hard to pray at times?
- In what area of your prayer life do you need to grow most?
- How can you help direct your child in prayer, starting today?

The Person Standing in Front of You

Karen

She had suffered a great deal under the care of many doctors and had spent all she had, yet instead of getting better she grew worse. When she heard about Jesus, she came up behind him in the crowd and touched his cloak, because she thought, "If I just touch his clothes, I will be healed."

—MARK 5:26–28

Mark 5 unfolds like a dramatic movie with a suspenseful plot. Jesus—who had been busy casting out demons, ministering to large crowds, and doing all that His Father commanded—heard that an important official had a young daughter who was at death's door. The official's name was Jairus, and he was the leader at the local synagogue.

Jesus responded to this desperate request and left to go meet the need. The crowds followed Him, anxious to see Him do this headliner miracle. However, Jesus' mission was interrupted. As the crowds pressed in around Him, a woman—who had suffered for twelve years with a medical issue and had gone to many doctors, spending a great deal of money with no improvement—was desperate to be healed. She reached out and touched Jesus in the midst of that crowd.

Jesus stopped and asked those standing around who had touched Him.

The disciples thought His question was a little crazy. How could He ask who had touched Him when so many people were pressing in all around? But the woman spoke up. Although she was afraid, she came forward. We see Jesus and her interacting, her faith having made her whole. The bleeding stopped. She was healed.

This encounter has always fascinated me. While on the way to perform a public miracle, Jesus allowed Himself to be interrupted. Although a public ministry with crowds around was what the people wanted to see, for Jesus, the real ministry was the person standing in front of Him: a person with an urgent need.

As mothers, we are busy women. We work. Volunteer. Help with projects at church. Often these commitments can seem so very important. But some days—as we are preparing to do something big—someone reaches out to us. It may be a child who is hurting. A neighbor who is struggling. A coworker who is grieving. At those times, will we do as Jesus did?

Our Lord often ministered to the person standing in front of Him. He took time. He listened. He touched. He engaged with the individual and met his or her need.

Who might stand in front of you today with a need, whether great or small? When they do, will you pause to help as Jesus did?

Father, help me have the perspective today that my greatest and most important ministry just may be to the person standing right in front of me. In Jesus' name, Amen.

- Can you think of a recent situation when you were on your way to do something big but were interrupted by someone who needed you? What happened?
- If the same situation were to happen today, would you handle it any differently? If so, how?

It's Okay to Ask for Help

Ruth

Let us not become weary in doing good, for at the proper time we will reap a harvest if we do not give up.

—Galatians 6:9

"Tyler, just a minute! I can't hear what you're saying!" I yelled in frustration.

I was upstairs in my youngest daughter's bedroom dealing with an unfolding drama that had me a bit frazzled. Surrounded by the whirlwind of emotions that to a six-year-old were very serious, I was at my wits' end. Not to mention my mind swirled with my looming list of things to be done at home.

I could hear Tyler calling my name from downstairs. He was trying to get my attention, but I couldn't hear him over the pitiful sobbing of my youngest. So in haste and anger I acted out, and almost as soon as the shout left my lips, I regretted it.

Tyler sheepishly replied, "Mom, I was just trying to tell you that a package came for you."

Sometimes—actually *lots* of times—in motherhood we feel overwhelmed and stretched beyond our capacity. Just taking care of our home is a round-the-clock job. That's why I learned many years ago that if I needed help, I had to ask for it. Bottom line. It's a myth to think that any mom can do and be all things, all the time!

With this in mind, I can breathe a deep sigh of relief as I ask for help during the different seasons when life feels a little chaotic. It's okay to ask for help. It isn't a weakness to need the help of a spouse, friend, or neighbor. God has gifted us with other people for a reason. In fact, I have come to realize that my own pride keeps others away from my need. I don't have to be a super mom to impress people or to seem like I have it all together. God has blessed us with one another to help carry the difficult and heavy burdens that different seasons bring.

For me, this means having a teenager from our church clean my house every other week. I also have someone play with the kids one morning each week so I can get a few hours of uninterrupted work done. Now, I really wish I had a full-time cook, but that might be taking it a little far!

What does asking for help look like for you? Whom can you invite into your life to help lift a heavy burden? None of us is meant to do life all alone. It's okay to ask for help!

Father, thank You for the strength and grace You supply me. Give me wisdom to know how I can let others help me when I'm weak or in need. Lord, You know where I'm struggling. Be my great Provider. In Jesus' name, Amen.

- What kinds of help do you wish you could ask for?
- In what areas of your life do you struggle to ask for help?
- If you aren't in a season of great need, are there other moms who could use your help?

Being Spiritually Sneaky

Karen

"But when you give to the needy, do not let your left hand know what your right hand is doing, so that your giving may be in secret. Then your Father, who sees what is done in secret, will reward you."

—MATTHEW 6:3–4

I love being a sneaky mom. And I've taken it upon myself to raise kids who are sneaky too. Now, by *sneaky,* I don't mean the kind of child who steals fresh-baked cookies from the cookie jar when you aren't looking or the teen who crawls out of his window at night to go hang out with his friends. I mean sneaky in a positive, spiritual sense.

In Scripture we find that Jesus commanded us to do good to others. To give to the needy. To help the downtrodden. To reach out to those less fortunate. But He didn't stop there; He also told us how to do it. We aren't to do good in order to draw attention to ourselves or elicit praise from others. In fact, Jesus encouraged us to be spiritually sneaky. He told us that we should give in secret. Then God our Father will see us and reward us.

We as a family have tried to adopt this practice and to work it naturally into our lives. My husband and I first began doing this two decades ago before we ever had children. We were continually on the lookout for someone who was having a rough time financially. They might get in their car after church and discover an envelope with a twenty-dollar bill in it, along with a note either to put it toward groceries or to use it to go out to lunch. (Twenty bucks went a long way back then!)

Once we had children, we let them in on the act. We encouraged them to be detectives, listening for someone who was sad, worried, or upset about something. Then, as a family, we would brainstorm ways we could—in secret—encourage and help that person. Over the years this has included leaving bags of groceries on someone's porch, tucking a gas or store gift card into someone's Bible at church when they weren't looking, or paying off a medical bill anonymously.

To help our children feel a part of the whole covert mission, we not only let them help pick who would be the recipient of our love, but we let them be a part of the gift. They get to shop for the groceries, pay the cashier for the gift cards, or be a part of the secret drop-off. Or they color pictures or make a homemade card to leave with our undercover offering.

How about your gang? Might you, too, become a family on a mission, Matthew 6:3–4 style? Your undercover kindness will not only bless those who receive your love, but it will encourage your own hearts as well. Try it this week. Sneaky can be fun and faith-filled!

Father, may I be on the lookout today for someone who needs a secret blessing from my family as a special touch from You. In Jesus' name, Amen.

- Think for a moment about an individual or family who might be in need financially or emotionally. What is one gesture you could do with your kids to secretly bless them? Talk with your family about this and plan to carry out your clandestine mission.

Letting Go of Anxiety

Ruth

When anxiety was great within me, your consolation brought me joy.

—Psalm 94:19

We were startled awake recently by the sound of one of our kids having a nightmare. Still in a fog myself, I ran into my daughter's room to console her.

It took longer than I expected to help her realize that her dream was just that—a dream. The line between nightmare and reality was a bit fuzzy for her.

Truthfully, that line gets fuzzy for us moms too. I know I can be a worrier. The fear of what might be can paralyze me if I let it. My guess is that this is true for most of us.

So where do we turn when this anxiousness wells up inside? My favorite place is the book of Psalms. I love the psalms because they are real life—real-life fear, real-life anger, real-life worry, real-life doubt. It's the stuff we all feel and try to make sense of.

And yet the psalmist rarely concludes with an emotion or feeling. Rather, he takes those feelings to the feet of God almost as a way of saying, "This is too big. Do something about this!"

And God always does. Like a parent who consoles a child, God graciously reminds us what reality is—even when our reality is scary, hard, or disappointing.

He takes us to His Word. Reminds us of His promises. Sings His love over us. Soothes us with His truth.

So what has been holding you back, keeping you up late at night, stealing your thoughts, and weighing heavy on your heart? What do you need to cast onto the God who cares for you beyond comprehension? He longs to sustain and guide you as you bring your life as an offering to Him.

Every moment that you clench tightly in desperate fear to control, God has it under control. Let go, my friend. He is with you right now.

If it's a hard place, He is there.

If it's a confusing place, He is there.

If it's a lonely place, He is there.

If it's a stressful place, He is there.

As a Father with infinite grace, wisdom, and power, He has not and will not leave you alone. Hold fast to Him.

Father, thank You for the reminder that You are near. Help me to know You and trust You. I cast my cares, my concerns, and the fears I have been carrying on You. Fill me with Your joy and with Your peace. In Jesus' name, Amen.

- What part of motherhood is most difficult to surrender to God right now?
- In what ways do you need God to comfort you? With His truth, His promises, or His love?
- How can you begin today to walk in faith instead of fear?

Embrace the Wait

Karen

I say to myself, "The LORD is my portion;
therefore I will wait for him."
—LAMENTATIONS 3:24

My three young kids were playing near her feet in her assisted-living home. "How busy things must be at your house these days. Why, I'd give anything to be able to spend an ordinary day with my children all little again. What joy!"

What joy? What was my husband's ninety-year-old grandmother talking about?! As a worn-out mom, I wanted the kids to get to the next stages in their lives, and fast! For one to walk, for another to stop wearing diapers, and for the third to learn to read. I wasn't joyful; I was anxious.

Now that two of my three kids have graduated from high school, I know what Grandma meant. I'd love to rewind the clock and experience one more ordinary day with my babies. If only I could make time wait instead of waiting on time to pass.

Even so, I still have a hard time applying this lesson in the midst of the wait. Each morning I wait in the school carpool line. In the afternoon, I wait for my son's football practice to wrap up. Sometimes the coach keeps the team after for a pep talk. Some days it's a lengthy one.

And so I sit. The minutes tick by, threatening to tick me off. You see, I don't like to wait.

Just this past week I waited in line at the grocery store, sat in the waiting room at the dentist's office, and lingered at the airport, anxious to board my plane. I also spent hours at the Department of Motor Vehicles so my son could get his driver's permit.

While these types of hindrances are short-lived, waiting for the next big thing can take longer and be harder. We wait for a house to sell, a child to take his first steps, a better job, financial relief, or physical or emotional healing to come to us or a loved one.

But Scripture teaches us how to make it through these difficult seasons. In those waiting times, even when life is hard, God says to us, *I'll be what you need while you wait.* God steps in to be our portion for that day. He is in the wait, and we'll sense that only if we look for Him rather than always looking ahead to the next stage of life.

He was my portion while I daydreamed about becoming a woman.

He was my portion when I waited to become a bride.

He was my portion as I longed to become a mom.

He was my portion as I looked forward to easier days.

The point of life is not to keep looking ahead, but to look to the Lord to be our portion at every stage of life.

Dear Lord, help me embrace the wait and look for You to be my portion during the in-between times of life. In Jesus' name, Amen.

→ What will you do to seek God as you wait? It gives meaning to the lingering and tethers your heart to His as you use these times to pray and ponder His goodness. Stop, take a deep breath, and do that right now.

Keep Growing with Others

Ruth

Let us consider how we may spur one another on toward love and good deeds, not giving up meeting together, as some are in the habit of doing, but encouraging one another—and all the more as you see the Day approaching.

—HEBREWS 10:24–25

Moms need other moms.

It's easy to become isolated with kids in the house. School, sports, extracurricular activities, work, taking care of the house, and so forth are all reasons for moms to cut out meaningful relationships with others. Though it may not seem like a big deal, disconnecting from others can have a huge impact on our emotional well-being, marriage, spiritual life, and role as a mom.

We need one another. We need to carve out time, as busy as motherhood can be. Getting together with other moms refuels us and helps us to keep pressing on!

No wonder this passage in Hebrews warns us about "giving up meeting together." Even at the time the writer wrote those words, some people were "in the habit of doing" just that. Apparently neglecting to get together is nothing new. So the writer warned against the dangers of trying to do life alone. But instead he wrote that we are to "spur one another on toward love and good deeds." We are to go on "encouraging one another," especially as the day of Christ's coming approaches.

It's too easy to grow weary, discouraged, or complacent in the

Christian life and in motherhood. We need others around us who are pursuing Christ to keep us pressing on during difficult times. We need the words of wisdom, accountability, correction, and encouragement that come with being in relationships with others.

Do you have that right now? Do you have other moms who have the permission to love you, hold you accountable, and even speak the truth when you need to hear it? We all need friends like that. They are God's gifts to us—especially during these years of motherhood when it's easy to go it alone.

We need to cultivate meaningful friendships with other women who are pursuing Jesus. Don't wait for the perfect friend to come to you; start by being one to another mom today. Pick up the phone. Send an e-mail. Invite someone over for coffee. Whatever you do, don't try to do life alone!

Father, thank You for the reminder that I need others in my life: friends who will love me, encourage me, and even hold me accountable. Help me be that kind of friend to others. And surround me with women who can cheer me on as I pursue You. In Jesus' name, Amen.

- Why is it so hard to cultivate meaningful friendships during motherhood?
- How has friendship with others helped you as a mom?
- How is God calling you to create and cultivate a stronger community with other moms? What do you need to do?

Last Things First

Karen

"So do not worry, saying, 'What shall we eat?' or 'What shall we drink?' or 'What shall we wear?' For the pagans run after all these things, and your heavenly Father knows that you need them. But seek first his kingdom and his righteousness, and all these things will be given to you as well."

—Matthew 6:31–33

As a woman and a mom, you wear a lot of hats. During the course of your week, you may place on your head any of the following hats: wife, mother, employee, daughter, sister, aunt, grandma, cook, bottle washer, chauffeur, nurse, maid, counselor, referee, PTA member, committee chair, and oh, yeah . . . and woman of God.

Sometimes these hats are stacked so high that trying to balance them all on our pretty little heads sends us toppling completely over! And, sadly, often the last hat we place on top is the crown we wear as a daughter of the King.

I love the simple, straight-shooting words of our Lord in Matthew 6. He cut to the chase, breaking commands down into bite-sized chunks. He outlined, gently but firmly, what we must do to get our lives in order: "Seek first his kingdom and his righteousness, and all these things will be given to you as well."

However simple these verses may be, fleshing them out in our lives isn't always easy, especially in our culture where frenzied activity breeds busyness. Years ago, success was determined by where you lived and what you drove. Now it seems that success is measured differently—by how busy you are.

We have no white space left on our calendar; our kids are carted from one activity to the next; why, we hardly even eat dinner as a family anymore. Something in us longs to "do more" by painting our lives in a bright, bold shade of busy.

Although we live in a much different time than the original hearers of Jesus' words, we can learn from them nonetheless. They were concerned about where their food and clothing would come from. While we may still have those concerns, there are other issues we fret over as well. Like how we will get the house cleaned, the kids bathed and dressed, the laundry done, the kids chauffeured, the marriage prioritized, the relative visited, the work project completed . . . and on and on.

While our tasks may shriek at us at every turn, Christ stands whispering, *Seek first My kingdom and My righteousness, and all these things will be given to you as well.*

Perhaps Jesus' words will prompt us to do a little hat-reduction, ridding our schedules of some of the activities that clamor for our attention and draw us away from time spent with Him.

Whatever hats God directs you to keep in your wardrobe, remember to don them in proper order. They will only stay standing when the crown you wear as a daughter of the King is placed on first!

Dear Lord, I'm sorry for the times when my hats are completely out of order. Every day may I seek You and Your righteousness first before I attempt to carry out any of my God-ordained responsibilities. In Jesus' name, Amen.

- What hats do you wear these days? List them. Now, prayerfully ask God if there are any that should go or at least be set aside for a time so that you are freer to focus on your priorities. Make this a matter of prayer today.

Mission as a Mom

Ruth

"You will receive power when the Holy Spirit comes on you; and you will be my witnesses in Jerusalem, and in all Judea and Samaria, and to the ends of the earth."

—Acts 1:8

We had seen each other numerous times at baseball games. Her son played on the same team as my son. This mom and I talked often, usually about the game, but occasionally the conversation would turn more personal. Our kids had caused our lives to intersect in ways they likely wouldn't have otherwise.

And then it hit me: a mission field, with many opportunities for minstry, is all around me as a mom. I'm not trapped in motherhood. I don't have to wait until my kids are grown to serve and live on mission. And in this season of motherhood, God has put a new mission field in front of me.

When kids come, serving and being involved in church can feel impossible. Lots of moms begin to view their family as their mission, which it certainly is. But we shouldn't stop there! God has placed other moms all around us. We have opportunities to make an impact for Christ in countless ways right now. We don't have to wait until the kids are grown.

Ministry doesn't have to be one more thing we add to an already busy schedule. What if we transformed the way we saw the places where God already has us? What if we began to see the people in our lives differently because of motherhood?

Recently a neighbor boy stopped by just before dinner, so we invited him to stay and eat with us. Aware of his background and family situation, we knew just the experience of sitting down to eat together was probably foreign to him. And so as a family, we were doing ministry together. Mission was happening at our dinner table.

Maybe it's at the park or during a conversation at a soccer game. Perhaps it's a trip to the zoo or another family at the store. This season of motherhood is full of unique potential. God wants to use you where you already are. He has put people in your life because you are a family that can be influential for Christ.

Motherhood is certainly ministry *to* your family, but it's also a means to ministry *as* a family!

Father, give me eyes to see the people You have placed in my life because of motherhood. Give me opportunities to share Your love and truth with them. Transform the way I see the people and places right in front of me. Give me courage to live on mission as a mom. In Jesus' name, Amen.

- What doors for spiritual conversations has motherhood opened for you?
- Who are a few people God has put on your heart to reach out to?
- Would you describe your perspective on motherhood as ministry *to* your family or ministry *as* a family?

____

____

____

____

About Karen Ehman

Karen Ehman is a Proverbs 31 Ministries speaker, a *New York Times* bestselling author, and a writer for Encouragement for Today, an online devotional that reaches more than 1 million women daily. She has written nine books, including *KEEP IT SHUT: What to Say, How to Say It & When to Say Nothing at All*. Married to her college sweetheart, Todd, and the mother of three, she enjoys antique hunting, cheering for the Detroit Tigers, and feeding those who gather around her kitchen island for a taste of Mama Karen's cooking. Connect with her at KarenEhman.com.

About Proverbs 31 Ministries

Karen Ehman is a *New York Times* bestselling author, speaker, and online devotion writer for Proverbs 31 Ministries, located in Charlotte, North Carolina.

If you were inspired by *Pressing Pause* and desire to deepen your own personal relationship with Jesus Christ, I encourage you to connect with Proverbs 31 Ministries. We exist to be a trusted friend who will take you by the hand and walk by your side, leading you one step closer to the heart of God through:

- First Five daily Bible study app
- Free online devotions
- Online Bible studies
- Daily radio programs
- Books and resources

For more information about Proverbs 31 Ministries, visit www.Proverbs31.org. To inquire about having Karen speak at your event, visit www.Proverbs31.org and click on "speakers."

About Ruth Schwenk

Ruth Schwenk is a pastor's wife, mom of four energetic kids, lover of coffee, and dreamer of big dreams. She is the creator of TheBetterMom.com, and along with her husband, Patrick, ForTheFamily.org. She is the coauthor of *Hoodwinked: Ten Myths Moms Believe and Why We All Need to Knock It Off*. A graduate of The Moody Bible Institute, Ruth and her husband have been in full-time local church ministry for more than fifteen years.

About The Better Mom

Now that you have learned how to reject the lies and start walking in the truth in this journey of motherhood, wouldn't it be great to connect with other moms? TheBetterMom.com is the place for you!

At The Better Mom our mission is to build God-honoring homes by inspiring moms to be better moms through sharing life and learning together. We are moms who desire to be "better" even though we are busy. We believe God has placed a high calling on our lives as we:

- Raise children to impact the world
- Take care of our homes
- Love our husbands
- Ultimately honor God with our lives

We would love to have you join our community and share in our journey! Join us today at www.TheBetterMom.com.